simply fresh

healthy made simple

from the kitchen of
Kylee Melo, R.D.

Simply Fresh: Healthy Made Simple
By Kylee Melo, R.D.

Content Copyright © 2017 by Kylee Melo
Design Copyright © 2017 by Typo Fire

Cover Design by Robert & Sara Koorenny
Layout Design by Ariel Warren
Food styling by Christin Miller
Photography by Nathan Bange
Text entry by Micheal Wardrip
Copy edited by Arlene Clark

Some health information was contributed
by Dr. Winston Craig

Second printing, 2019

Images on pages 12, 15, 16 are used with
permission.

Icon vector graphics used for health
benefits are from www.vecteezy.com

Published by Typo Fire
Printed in the U.S.A.
www.typofire.com/books

ISBN 13: 978-0-9851702-1-9

Nutritional information provided was
calculated using software-generated
averages, and may vary based on the
brands or specific ingredients you use.

This book is not intended to diagnose or
treat any medical conditions. The author
assumes full responsibility for the accuracy
of all facts and quotations as cited in
this book. Consult your physician before
beginning a diet plan.

For those who helped guide me along the way, I thank you. My mom, Jenny, who made my sister and I take turns cooking on nights she worked. My dad, Kip, for only knowing how to make waffles and toast, which encouraged us to learn how to cook. My sister, Tara, who is a professional cook, and an inspiration of what hard work and dedication looks like. My nephew, Kian, for loving my Pumpkin Cheesecake "Ky Ky's Pie", more than any other dessert. My favorite professor, Dr. Winston Craig, for seeing the potential in me when no one else did. My husband, Paulo (the grestest man I ever met),

for encouraging me to follow my passion as God leads. Finally, my soon-to-be-born son, Benjamin Clifford Melo, who made me want to accomplish more than I could imagine, and who will teach me to look to God for guidance in every situation.

This book could not have been completed without help from Upper Columbia Conference, and literature evangelists from around the country. Thanks to Nathan Bange and Christin Miller for the beautiful photography and gorgeous food styling, Sara Koorenny for recommending me to write the book, and her wonderful husband, Robert Koorenny, who coordinated getting this cookbook put together.

Contents

Breakfast   20

Start off Right: The best way to start the day is by eating a balanced breakfast. It should be the biggest meal of the day, so don't hold back here!

Sides   34

Not Just on the Side: Side dishes can even be used as main dishes for a lighter meal, or can be a perfect way to add variety alongside another dish.

Salad   40

Power Up: There are plenty of ways to make sure you are getting enough veggies in your daily diet. Try these salads for a great addition to your meal.

HOW TO USE THE GUIDES:

The icons and descriptions below show you how to improve areas of your life just by eating the right foods! Use the key to help you identify which recipes help with various aspects of your health. In the back of this book, you will also find a special index that directs you to all the recipes that pertain to that benefit (starting on page 121).

Basics 102

Healthy Staples: Enjoy a new way to eat traditional sauces and condiments. There's nothing basic about the way these recipes taste!

Drinks & Juicing 108

Refresh Yourself: Drink to health with these amazingly flavorful drinks and juices. Enjoy a quick way to add many nutrients to your daily diet.

HEALTH BENEFIT

- Reduces Inflammation
- Good for Digestion
- Heart Healthy
- Good for Kidneys
- Nervous system +
- Lowers Cholesterol
- Good for the Arteries
- Good for the Skin
- Immunity Boost
- Cancer Fighting

SPECIAL DIET

- (GF) Gluten Free
- (NF) Nut Free
- (SF) Soy Free
- (D) Diabetic Friendly

Health & Happiness

Health and wellness aren't just about diet, although what you eat plays a big part in how long you're likely to live. In this introduction, you'll read about the main factors that can help you live a long and healthy life.

LONGEVITY & THE BLUE ZONES

The world's longevity all-stars live healthy, active lives well into their 90s and 100s. Yes, they not only live longer, but they also retain their vitality well into old age. Places where there exist a high percentage of centenarians in the population are designated Blue Zones. Longevity experts identified five Blue Zones in the world – Sardinia, Italy; Ikaria, Greece; Okinawa, Japan; Loma Linda, California; and the Nicoya peninsula in Costa Rica. Their secrets to a long life were discovered, not in pills or surgery, but in the everyday things that they do, such as the foods they eat and the company they keep.

In his book "The Blue Zones," Buettner describes a number of common features that characterize people living in the Blue Zones. The inhabitants of these areas engage in low-intensity physical activity as part of their usual work routine. They were observed to walk every day. This includes a combination of aerobic and muscle-strengthening activities to ensure good body balance.

Longevity all-stars also did not overeat. They ate to satisfy hunger rather than eating until they felt full. They typically ate nutrient-dense foods rather than calorie-dense foods. It was noted that the Okinawan stir-fried tofu and greens has the same volume as a hamburger and fries, but the Okinawan meal has only one-fifth the calories. In the Blue Zones, the biggest meal of the day is typically eaten during the first half of the day and typically plant-based foods are eaten. They often eat food from their own gardens rather than processed foods, soda pop, or salty snacks. Whole grains, beans (or tofu), and garden vegetables are the cornerstone of all Blue Zone diets. A significant number of Adventists in Loma Linda, California are vegetarian or near-vegetarian.

In his study of the centenarians, Buettner describes the inhabitants of the Blue Zones as happy people, possessing a strong sense of purpose and a clear goal in life, which gave them fulfillment and meaning. They have time periods where they slow down, unwind and de-stress. The most successful centenarians also put families first. They make family time a real priority.

Healthy people who live to 100 years and beyond possess faith and participate in a spiritual community that fosters social networks and connectedness. Religion typically encourages positive expectations that improves health. Seventh-day Adventists were the subjects of the research conducted in the Loma Linda, California, Blue Zone. Buettner observed the positive outlook on life among the Loma Linda centenarians and their strong community life. He was particularly fascinated by their observance of the Sabbath from sundown Friday to sundown Saturday. In this sanctuary of time, normal work ceased and the day was spent in worship, outdoor nature walks, relaxing, and interacting with family.

Buettner observed that the centenarians surrounded themselves with people who share the same Blue Zone values as themselves. It is easier, he says, to adopt good health habits when you hang out with people who are practicing those things. By adopting the lifestyle habits of Blue Zone inhabitants we also can live longer and improve the quality of our lives. Let's explore some of those habits.

BREAKFAST

Breakfast literally means "breaking the fast." You have been fasting for more than 7 hours, so it's important to start your day off with a healthy breakfast. It is the foundation for optimal physical and intellectual performance.

Not only does it provide us with energy, but breakfast foods contain important nutrients such as calcium, protein, fiber, iron, and B vitamins. By skipping breakfast it is easy to miss out on these essential nutrients, and it is less likely to be compensated for later in the day.

Some think that by skipping breakfast you will be cutting out calories, however, studies have shown that those who skip breakfast are more likely to reach for high sugar and fatty snacks mid-morning. There are many observational studies that have found people who skip breakfast are more likely to be overweight.

Breakfast helps with better learning in the classroom or workroom. There tends to be less accidents and better concentration in those who eat breakfast. There is a faster reaction time and less mid-morning fatigue. So a better way to stay awake and alert in the mornings is to reach for breakfast instead of the coffee, and it will work to your benefit in many ways!

Make sure you are eating a well-balanced breakfast daily. Choosing whole grains, nuts and fruits is always a great option for a healthy way to start the day.

Eating a healthy breakfast can help with lowering cholesterol levels, improved performance and concentration, and helps create a more nutritionally complete diet.

WEIGHT & CALORIES

There are plenty of weight loss programs and products promising rapid weight loss, or the perfect bikini body in a hurry. Over 89 billion dollars are spent on diets and supplements each year. Yet we are still one of the most obese countries in the world. For the most part, these do not work, especially in the long run. It has become a huge money making industry that leads people to believe they can lose weight in a hurry.

Many have tried these fad diets or products! Was there weight loss? Probably—in the beginning or while adhering to the plan—because, as with any diet that restricts calories or nutrients, they make anyone lose weight. How long does the weight stay off? Is it healthy to lose weight so quickly?

Side effects of rapid weight loss can include:

Hair loss, muscle loss, headaches, irritability, fatigue, constipation, dizziness, menstrual irregularities, and can lead to gallstones, dehydration, malnutrition and electrolyte imbalance.

By and large, diets are not adhered to by the majority of people. If 100 people start a diet, within seven to ten months 90 of those people will quit. Within the next 2 years all but about 5 will quit the program.

When it comes to weight loss or weight

management it is important to make changes that can last a lifetime. It's not about low-calorie restricted diets, creams, diet supplements, or magic voodoo spells. Rather it's about sustaining a healthy lifestyle for a lifetime.

A healthy weight loss is considered to be 0.5-2 pounds lost per week. Slow and steady wins the race. When weight comes off quickly, it typically comes back quickly. When it comes off slowly by exercising and eating better, it's much more likely to be kept off for the long haul.

The best way to lose weight is by daily exercising and healthy eating. This doesn't mean eating a bowl of salad at each meal, but rather choosing foods that are rich in nutrients and fiber. Foods that will bring health, healing and are a pleasure to eat.

Balancing calories consumed and calories used is how to properly maintain weight. The key to weight management is to prevent gradual weight gain over time. Making small changes to decrease calories and increase physical activity prevents weight gain. Childhood is where healthful eating and regular physical activity should begin.

For those who are overweight or obese, losing 7% body weight helps to lower the risk of many diseases. For example, if a person weighs 200 pounds and wants to lose 7% body weight to live a healthier life, this is equal to a 14-pound weight loss.

WATER

How much water is enough water to drink per day? Is it 6, 8, 10 cups a day? An easy way to figure out how much water you should be drinking is to take your weight in pounds and divide it in half. This will give you an approximate number of ounces to drink during the day.

Water is especially important when you are increasing your daily fiber intake. If you are increasing fiber without increasing water intake, you may still be fighting constipation.

Try drinking water first thing in the morning when you wake up. Put a glass of water next to your bed at night, as a reminder for when you wake up in

the morning. Your body has gone 7-9 hours without having any liquids so it is dehydrated and needs to be re-hydrated with water. Reach for a nice tall glass of water before reaching for anything else.

Sometimes, shortly after we finish our meal, we start to feel a bit hungry. Instead of reaching for

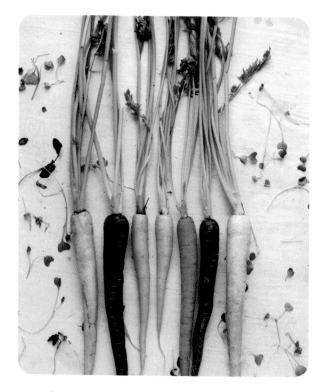

something else to eat, reach for a glass of water. We start feeling hungry when really we are thirsty. If you drink a glass of water you will start to feel full or satisfied again. Give it a try!

Why are we so used to drinking something with our meals? At restaurants they always ask you what you would like to drink with your meal. This is one bad habit that has become the norm. The best time to drink something is before a meal or an hour or more after your meal. This is due to the process of digestion. Digestion begins in the mouth as our saliva comes together with our food. Our saliva contains enzymes that aid in the breakdown of food, and this covers the pieces of food in our mouth. It then continues being digested and broken down all the way from the mouth through the colon. When we drink liquid with our food, the liquid then dilutes those digestive enzymes and hormones that are produced in the digestive system.

The total amount of fiber consumed should be around 30-40 grams per day. The average American consumes around 15 grams a day. Foods that contain fiber are fruits, vegetables, whole grains, nuts, seeds, and legumes.

A great way to increase fiber is to add a ½ cup of beans to your largest meal. Research has shown beans help to keep the blood sugars more stable for several hours. Say you eat a ½ cup of beans with your lunch today, your blood sugars could be lower after your dinner because of the beans you ate at lunch time. Beans are a low glycemic food, which means they do not increase the blood sugars much. Beans contain fiber and resistant starch which increases colonic fermentation (gut bacteria). This keeps our blood sugars lower for longer periods of time.

Increase your fruits and vegetables intake. Fruits and vegetables are typically low in calories and high in nutrients and fiber. Make sure to get 5 plus cups of fruits and vegetables a day.

Whole food fats are the way to go! These would include nuts, seeds, olives, avocados and coconut. These are the healthy type of fats that naturally occur in plant-based foods.

Taking a leisurely walk after a meal can help lower your blood sugars from 1-3 points per minute spent walking. Say you walk for 15 minutes after your meal. This can help lower your blood sugars 15-45 points. This can add up quickly and intensely decrease the damage that can occur from after-meal blood sugar spikes.

Cut down on or out the soft drinks and other caloric liquids. These tend to be high in calories and sugar, which will make the blood sugars spike quickly. Choose water in place of these drinks, or try a sparkling naturally flavored water when craving a soft drink.

For those who are concerned, the best and most accurate way to see if you are pre-diabetic or type 2 diabetic is to have your hemoglobin A1C checked. It's important to ask your doctor to run this test along with your other blood work.

Inflammation is the body's reaction for healing itself. The body was created to self-protect against harmful stimuli. When you get a small cut usually there are no drastic measures you need to take since the body automatically goes to work and starts the healing process. When something irritating or harmful affects a part of the body, there is a natural biological response to start removing it. Signs and symptoms of this can appear as inflammation, specifically acute inflammation. This is a good sign because it means the body is attempting to defend itself from bacteria, viruses, foreign invaders, or after an injury. However, inflammation can cause more inflammation, which can become chronic.

Chronic inflammation has been linked to heart disease, diabetes, lung issues, bone health, cancer, depression, and chronic joint pain. It is not only injury or foreign invaders that cause inflammation, but foods can cause inflammation as well. This is why it is helpful to be aware of the foods you choose, because some increase inflammation in the body, while others can help to decrease it.

Following an anti-inflammatory diet can reduce the risk of these diseases. It reduces blood triglycerides and blood pressure, and soothes tender and stiff arthritic joints.

What to do:

- Eat plenty of fruits and vegetables
- Eat plant sources of omega-3 fatty acids, such as walnuts, flaxseed or chia seed
- Eat plenty of whole grains
- Avoid refined and processed foods
- Use turmeric, ginger, curry and other spices, which are anti-inflammatory
- Get about 3 grams or more a day of omega -3 fatty-acids (flaxseed, chia seed)

Foods to avoid:

Meat, pork, alcoholic beverages, milk, egg, additives (coloring agents)

Anti-inflammatory foods:

Fruits, legumes, beets, garlic, soy, vegetables, nuts, ginger, whole grains, turmeric, walnuts.

LOWERING BLOOD PRESSURE

Blood pressure readings include a combination of the systolic (the top number) and diastolic (the bottom number). The systolic blood pressure refers to the force of the blood being pushed through the arteries to the rest of the body. The normal number for this is 120 or below. The diastolic blood pressure is the force of blood flow in the arteries when the heart rests between beats, and the heart fills with blood. A normal reading for the diastolic is 80 or below. Below is a more detailed chart on the reading of blood pressure results.

Category	Systolic / Diastolic
Low	<80 / <60
Normal	80-120 / 60-79
Pre-hypertension	120-139 / 80-89
Hypertension I	140-159 / 90-99
Hypertension II	>160 / >100
Crisis (seek emergency care)	>180 / >110

Think of high blood pressure this way: a garden hose in your yard works like the arteries. When the water is on and flowing nicely, there are no issues. If you put your thumb over the nozzle, you'll notice the water begins to come out with a higher amount of force. Having too much water pressure in the hose can cause damage to the hose. When the blood pressure is high, the arteries are similarly working like the hose with your thumb covering some of the nozzle. It can cause damage to the arteries and lead to heart disease and stroke.

There are many ways you can naturally help to lower your blood pressure through diet and a healthy lifestyle. Below are some tips to help lower your blood pressure, and therefore lower your risk of stroke or heart disease.

Healthy Eating:

Consume a dietary pattern that emphasizes intake of vegetables, fruits, and whole grains, non-tropical vegetable oils and nuts.

Avoid the use of these food or nutrients:

High sodium foods, ham, sausages, meats, alcoholic beverages, saturated fat, coffee, caffeinated beverages, and matured cheeses.

Lower sodium intake:

Consume no more than 2,400 mg of sodium per day, which equates to about 1 teaspoon. Reducing sodium intake further to 1,500 mg/day is desirable since it is associated with even greater reduction in blood pressure. Those who are more at risk for high blood pressure include African-Americans, the elderly, and those with high blood pressure. Reducing intake by at least 1,000 mg/day will help to lower blood pressure

The DASH (Dietary Approaches to Stop Hypertension) dietary pattern is high in vegetables, fruits, low-fat dairy products, whole grains, poultry, fish, and nuts; and it is low in sweets, sugar-sweetened beverages, and red meat. The DASH dietary pattern is also low in saturated fat, total fat, and cholesterol. It is rich in potassium, magnesium, and calcium, as well as protein and fiber.

How to reduce the salt in your diet:

Choose packaged and prepared foods carefully. Compare labels and choose the product with the lowest amount of sodium (per serving) you can find in your store. You might be surprised that different brands of the same food can have different sodium levels. Try to avoid processed or boxed foods as much as possible. Choose low-salt or salt-reduced products when possible.

Choose condiments carefully. For example, soy sauce, bottled salad dressings, dips, ketchup, jarred salsas, capers, mustard, pickles, olives and relish can be very high in sodium. Choose a reduced or lower-sodium version if available, or make your own from the recipes provided in this cookbook.

Choose canned vegetables labeled "no salt added" and frozen vegetables without salty sauces. When adding these to dishes, soups, or other items there will be other ingredients involved which helps the tastebuds to not miss the salt. Drain off the liquid and discard when using cans with salt added.

When preparing food:

Instead of using salt to flavor food, try using onions, garlic, herbs, spices, citrus juices and vinegars in place of some or all of the salt to add flavor to foods.

Drain and rinse canned beans (chickpeas, kidney beans, etc.) and vegetables – this can help cut the sodium by up to 40 percent.

Cook pasta, rice, and hot cereal without salt. There are many other flavors to add to these foods, so the salt will not be missed.

Cook by grilling, braising, roasting, searing, and sautéing to bring out the natural flavors in foods.

Incorporate foods with potassium. Foods like sweet potatoes, potatoes, greens, tomatoes, white beans, kidney beans, oranges, bananas and cantaloupe. Potassium helps to counter the effects of sodium and may help to lower blood pressure.

The American Heart Association's (AHA) website has more information on lowering blood pressure.

LOWERING CHOLESTEROL

Cholesterol is naturally found in the body. It is primarily produced in the liver, and a small amount is made by individual cells in the body and the lining of the small intestine. The body produces the amount of cholesterol it needs, so adding more can be harmful and life threatening.

Cholesterol is found in animal-based food and is an undesirable element. Plant-based foods, on the other hand, do not contain cholesterol.

Total cholesterol correlates with the risk for cardiovascular disease. An excess amount of cholesterol can cause a hardening or narrowing of the arteries, which increases the risk of a stroke or heart attack.

The ideal amount of daily intake of cholesterol would be 0 mg per day, but the acceptable daily intake for a healthy adult is 300 mg or less, according to the AHA. For those with diabetes, high cholesterol or heart disease, this daily limit should be no more than 200 mg a day.

Be aware that one egg contains almost the total amount of cholesterol that is recommended for the entire day. An egg contains about 213 mg of cholesterol. How many people only eat one egg at a time? Typically, people eat 2-3 eggs at a time, and that's not including the rest of the milk, cheese, other dairy products, or meat that they eat during the rest of the day! Below are the blood level ranges for cholesterol.

Total Cholesterol	US (mg/dL)
Normal	<200 mg
Borderline High	200-239 mg
High	>240 mg

Regardless of whether you are planning on including drug therapy or not, you can do a number of things every day to improve your cholesterol levels and your overall health.

Eat a heart-healthy diet by emphasizing fruits, vegetables, whole grains, legumes, and nuts in your diet.

Limit the intake of foods that contain cholesterol, such as: pork, beef, chicken, turkey, fish, dairy products, eggs, and cheese.

Get moving! Just 40 minutes of aerobic exercise of moderate to vigorous intensity done 3-4 times a week is enough to lower both cholesterol and high blood pressure. Brisk walking, swimming, bicycling or a dance class are some examples.

Avoid tobacco smoke. If you smoke, your cholesterol level is one more good reason to quit. Everyone should avoid exposure to secondhand smoke, too.

Eating a healthy diet and including exercise in your routine can give you the edge in the fight against heart disease and stroke.

LOWERING TRIGLYCERIDES

Triglycerides are a type of fat (lipid) that is found in the blood. They are used for energy and they are needed for good health. However, when the triglycerides are high, it increases the risk of heart disease. The body converts unused calories, that are not needed right away, into triglycerides. If excess calories are eaten, this can cause high triglycerides. Below are some tips to reduce your triglycerides.

Moderate exercise on 5 or more days each week can help lower triglyceride levels. Aim for 30 minutes each day.

Losing 5%-10% of your weight can lower triglycerides. People with a healthy weight are more likely to have normal triglyceride levels. Belly fat is associated with higher levels. There are many other benefits of losing weight so focus on those, such as improved health, increased energy, and feeling better.

Reducing saturated fat, trans fat, and cholesterol in your diet can improve triglyceride levels and help manage cholesterol. It helps to trade plant fats for animal fats, so try using olive oil, canola oil, avocados, olives, etc.

Drinking alcohol can increase triglyceride levels. Some studies show that drinking more than one drink a day for women or two for men can raise triglyceride levels a lot. Cutting out alcohol entirely may be necessary for some people with high triglycerides.

Eating more foods rich in omega-3s can lower triglyceride levels. Ground flaxseed or chia seed is a great way to get the omega-3s. Other good foods to eat that lower triglycerides are soy, beans, avocado, onion, guava, wheat germ, and flaxseed.

LOWERING LDL "BAD" CHOLESTEROL

Low-density lipoprotein (LDL) cholesterol is referred to as the "bad" cholesterol. This is because when there is too much in the blood it can cause plaque buildup in the arteries and result in stroke and heart disease.

Consume a dietary pattern that emphasizes intake of vegetables, fruits, and whole grains; legumes, non-tropical vegetable oils and nuts; and limits intake of sweets, sugar-sweetened beverages and red meats.

Aim for a dietary pattern that achieves 5% to 6% of calories from saturated fat.

Reduce your percentage of calories from saturated fat, and eliminate calories from trans-fat.

Engage in aerobic physical activity. Get 3 to 4 sessions a week, lasting on average 40 minutes per session, and involving moderate-to-vigorous intensity physical activity.

RAISING HDL "GOOD" CHOLESTEROL

High-density lipoprotein (HDL) is what usually referred to as "good" cholesterol. That's because it picks up the excess cholesterol in the blood and takes it back to the liver where it is broken down and removed from the body. It's clear why it is referred to as the "good" cholesterol. Here are a few tips on how to raise your HDL cholesterol:

Lower weight if you are overweight.

Increase physical activity. Benefits can be seen with as little as 60 minutes of moderate intensity aerobic exercise a week.

Eat good fats like nuts, flaxseed, olive, or avocados.

Stop smoking.

CREATING A HEALTHY KITCHEN

Get the healthy kitchen makeover that you deserve and need. Not all of these products are necessary, so it may help to choose a few of them to get started. With time, your pantry will change into a healthy environment for the whole family.

Refrigerator: A great tip is to keep fresh fruits and vegetables on the top shelf of the fridge, or the shelf that is eye level. This way the eye goes straight to those fresh foods.

Fruits: Grapes, berries, cherries, plums, cut fruit

Vegetables: Lettuce, asparagus, broccoli, leafy greens, cabbage, spinach, bell peppers, cauliflower, carrots, celery, avocado, fresh mushrooms

Herbs: Cilantro, parsley, basil, rosemary, thyme, dill

Others: Tofu, veggie meats, dairy-free milk, dairy-free butter, hummus, ground flaxseed, olives, Bragg's Liquid Aminos (or low sodium soy sauce), pure vanilla extract, liquid smoke.

Freezer: When storing food in the freezer there are a couple of tips to keep in mind. 1. Food should be tightly wrapped in multiple layers to prevent freezer burn. 2. Make sure the air is out of the packaging. 3. Allow space in your freezer, versus jamming it packed full. This helps the air to circulate to keep it at the ideal temperature.

Frozen peas, frozen corn, frozen bananas (unpeeled and in a freezer bag), frozen fruits for smoothies, whole grain bread, vegetable medley, frozen soups, frozen edamame.

Pantry: These plant-based foods are staple foods for a healthy, hearty kitchen. Be sure to keep plenty of these on hand at all times.

Legumes: dried black beans, dried pinto beans, lentils, great northern beans, red lentils, kidney beans.

Grains: Quinoa, brown rice, quick oats, old fashioned oats, wild rice, whole grain pastas, whole wheat tortilla, whole grain bread

Vegetables & Fruits: Onions, garlic, potatoes, sweet potatoes, squash, lemons, limes, mangoes, oranges, apples, pears, bananas, avocados

Sauces: extra virgin olive oil, canola oil, extra virgin olive oil cooking spray, low sodium spaghetti sauce

Canned Foods: Vegetable broth, canned coconut milk, low-sodium canned beans, artichoke hearts, heart of palm

Nuts, Seeds, & Dried Fruit: Raw cashews, raw almonds, peanuts, raw walnuts, flaxseed, chia seeds, sunflower seeds, sesame seeds, almond butter, peanut butter, raisins, cranberries, dates

Seasonings & Spices: Turmeric, McKay's chicken and beef seasonings, nutritional yeast flakes, baking soda, aluminum-free baking powder, cinnamon, pumpkin pie spice, apple pie spice, sea salt, cayenne, garlic powder, onion powder, bay leaves, basil, oregano, paprika, unsweetened cocoa powder, curry powder, ginger.

INCREASING WHOLE GRAIN INTAKE

Whole grains are the natural way that wheat and grains are grown. It wasn't until the 19th century that people began to make white flour. A grain of wheat contains the bran, endosperm, and germ. Bran is rich in fiber, vitamins and minerals. The bran is the part of the wheat that has cholesterol lowering properties, due to its fiber. The starch and proteins of the grain are from the endosperm or nucleus. The germ of the wheat is very rich in B and E vitamins.

White flour is taking out the bran and germ

from the wheat. When eating white bread or other products containing white flour, you are losing out on the fiber, B vitamins, and E vitamins. White products tend to make the blood sugars rise due to their lack of fiber.

The fiber in whole grains helps give a more satisfying sense of fullness, because of the fiber content. The fiber swells in the stomach, giving a full feeling, which helps you eat less, thus helping to prevent obesity.

Due to the antioxidants, unsaturated fatty acids, trace elements, phytochemicals and fiber, they help to avoid heart disease and plaque build-up of the arteries.

Studies have demonstrated that the more whole grain products that are eaten, the lower the risk of type 2 diabetes. Diabetics tolerate whole grains much more than refined grains, due to the glucose in whole grains releasing slowly. There is not an abrupt increase in the blood levels, unlike refined grain products.

Whole grains can include bread, pasta, brown rice, popcorn, flakes, puffed cereals, some breakfast cereals, oats, barley, bran, rye, millet, spelt, kamut, sorghum, corn, and wild rice.

EXERCISE

We all know it's important to get adequate exercise, but that doesn't mean we always do. Benefits to exercise are that it helps to control weight, helps combat health conditions, improves mood, boosts energy, and it helps to have better sleep.

Exercise is a great way to maintain or lose weight. It burns off extra calories, which can help to maintain weight. Or if enough calories are being burned during exercise and calories consumed are within a reasonable amount, weight loss is experienced.

One of the best forms of exercise is walking. It's free, easy on the body, and something most of us do each day. Make an effort to walk more during the day. Keep track of how many steps you are taking a day. A good daily goal would be 10,000 steps. You may need to work up to this amount, or you may be reaching this goal already.

A leisurely walk after a meal can be very beneficial in so many ways. Studies are finding that by taking a stroll after a meal blood sugars can be reduced by 1-3 points for every minute spent walking after a meal. Blood sugars tend to be highest 45-60 minutes after eating, so going for a leisurely walk can help to reduce those numbers. It can help to lower triglycerides, aids in digestion, prevents food coma, and helps control weight.

A good weekly target would be to aim for at least 150 minutes of moderate-intensity exercise. There are many types of exercise to choose from, so find some you enjoy. Walking, running, swimming, sports, group aerobic classes, lifting weights, yoga, and much more.

THE TRUTH ABOUT CARBOHYDRATES

A lot of fad diets encourage people to stay away from carbohydrates, or to eat a small amount of them. Did you know the body needs carbohydrates to function properly? Carbohydrates (carbs) are transformed into energy to keep us running and are the primary source of energy for the body. Our brains rely on carbohydrates; it is what feeds them. Carbs are broken down into glucose, which is what is used to fuel the brain. If there is a lack of carbs in the diet then protein is broken down into glycogen, which the brain then uses, but not as proficiently as glucose.

No-carb or low-carb diets have been linked to impairment of memory in studies. After one week, those on a low-carb diet performed worse on memory-based tasks than those following a diet consisting mostly of fruits, vegetables and whole grains. The conclusion of the study was that a low-carb diet can be detrimental to learning, memory, and thinking.

Not all carbohydrates are the same. There are refined and whole grains. Refined, or simple, carbs tend to give our bodies a rapid jolt of energy, which fades away and leave us feeling lethargic. Whole grains, or complex carbohydrates, provide energy that is more sustained strength and energy. Whole grains contain fiber, which helps to keep the blood sugars from spiking, whereas refined carbs tend to spike the blood sugars, and increases the risk of diabetes.

Fruits contain carbohydrates as well, and some diets warn against eating them for this reason. This is a huge detriment to health. Fruits contain great amounts of nutrients and antioxidants that are

important for the body and the immune system. Fruits are also a great natural dessert to help curb the sweet tooth. Not only fad diets, but people with diabetes have been told to avoid fruits. Another big mistake! Eating too many fruits can spike the blood sugar, which is why it is important not to overdo it, as with any type of food.

Stop and think about what foods would bring healing to the body. We know fruits and vegetables are great sources of antioxidants, which help fight against disease. Whole grains contain fiber which also helps to fight against disease. These contain carbohydrates and yet the help to fight against disease of the body. Any diet that is suggesting to stay away from foods like these are probably just after the money, rather than wanting to bring health and healing.

FIBER

It's important to make sure you are eating enough fiber on a daily basis. Fiber helps to normalize bowel movements, maintain bowel health, lower cholesterol levels, control blood sugar levels, and helps in achieving a healthy weight.

Fiber is the part of the plant that the body is not able to digest or absorb. It is the roughage or bulk of the plant. It passes through the stomach and bowels relatively intact, and exits the body. A lot of fiber is degraded by the colonic flora and alters the microbiome which influences risk of disease.

It is found only in plant-based foods: fruits, vegetables, whole grains, nuts, seeds and beans. Meats, eggs and dairy do not contain any fiber. So when people load up on bacon and eggs for breakfast, steak or chicken for lunch and dinner, they are getting zero fiber.

The average adult eats only 15 grams of fiber per day, while the recommendation for women is 25 grams, and 38 grams a day for men, according to the Institute of Medicine. Yet even better than this is getting around 40 grams per day.

Inadequate fiber intake can lead to constipation, which may cause other health issues. Hemorrhoids, anal fissures, and colonic conditions are some of the complications of constipation.

Make sure you are choosing plenty of high fiber plant-based foods to ensure healthy and regular bowel movements. Cereal fiber is different from vegetable and fruit fiber. Each has a part to play in our health.

HEALTHY FATS

Fats are necessary for the body to function normally. They help to transport and absorb the fat-soluble vitamins A, D, E, and K, vitamins that are essential for good health.

Fats are found in both animal and plant-based foods. There are better types of fats than others, which is why it is important to choose the healthier types of fat, and enjoy them in moderation. Nuts, seeds, avocados, olive, and coconut are all natural plant-based foods that contain fat. These fats have special protective nutrients that the body needs. The advantage of plant-based fats is they are in a natural state, they tend to have little fat, and they're predominately unsaturated fats, which help to reduce blood cholesterol levels. Unsaturated fats are the ideal fats to eat, especially when they come from whole plant-based foods.

Animal-based foods tend to be high in fats, whether from meats or dairy products, unless made into low-fat or from a lean cut meat. A great amount of fat comes from saturated fats, which increase cholesterol production of the body. Not only do they contain saturated fat, but also cholesterol which can contribute to heart disease.

Saturated fats are found in meats, poultry, lard, egg yolks, whole-fat dairy products, and tropical oils including coconut and palm oils. Lowering or replacing foods high in saturated fat with healthier options can help to lower blood cholesterol levels.

Trans-fats are found in vegetables—fats that are hardened, such as margarine and vegetables shortening. There are plenty of foods that contain these ingredients such as cookies, crackers, cakes, pies, baked goods, candies, French fries, and other snack foods. It is important to abstain from trans-fatty foods. Trans-fats raise bad (LDL) and decrease good (HDL) cholesterol. They can increase the risk of developing heart disease and stroke. There is also a high risk for developing type 2 diabetes when consuming foods that contain trans-fat.

Fat is high in calories, which is why it is important to stick to a good-health portion. Excess fat can lead to becoming overweight when eaten in abundance, no matter where the fat comes from. It is recommended that less than 30% of the daily calories come from fat, that's less than 65 grams of fat per day. Some healthy foods that contain fat are nut milks, tofu, oats avocados, coconut, nuts, seeds, and olives.

FAITH AND YOUR HEALTH

Research studies conducted at leading universities have shown that religious beliefs and practices are positively associated with one's mental health and physical well-being. Over 600 studies now provide evidence that individuals who attend religious services on a regular basis, who have a meaningful religious experience, and who are committed to their faith have fewer health problems. They have better mental health, greater social support, and live healthier lifestyles. This means that those who live their faith can enjoy better physical health. And what results do they see? Such people have fewer visits to the doctor, they are more likely to recover faster from an illness, they have shorter hospital stays, have better surgical outcomes, expend less for health care, and have a greater survival rate.

Furthermore, those who attend church regularly have greater marital satisfaction, less anxiety over their problems, and less depression. People with a strong religious commitment not only suffer less depression but show a 70 percent speedier recovery from depression. Religious involvement also reduces risky health behaviors, including a reduced alcohol and drug use. Furthermore, a belief that the body is the temple of God will encourage a person to develop a healthier lifestyle.

Religious belief can also affect health outcomes. In heart patients, Dr. Morris observed that those who scored the lowest on a spiritual well-being questionnaire experienced the most progression of coronary blockage over four years, while those with the highest scores of spiritual well-being had the most regression of heart disease. In patients recently diagnosed with HIV infection, an increased level of spirituality of the patient predicted a slower progression of the disease.

People who attend religious services and pray or study the Bible were 40 percent less likely to have elevated blood pressure, and hence a lowered risk of stroke. Studies found that patients who had open-heart surgery and who received solace and comfort from their religious beliefs were three times more likely to survive than those who did not have a religious faith. Women of religious faith who had hip surgery were able to walk again sooner after their surgery than other women.

Religious belief, prayer, and meditation may also be important strategies that help people cope with a medical illness or handle a major stress in their life, rather than turning to negative health behaviors. Religious belief provides a person with an optimistic worldview, infusing purpose and meaning into difficult life situations. Such attitudes are associated with an increased chance of one's survival rate.

In a recent review of 850 studies on the relationship between religion and mental health, the majority of the studies revealed that higher levels of religious involvement were positively associated with indicators of better mental health and psychological well-being, such as satisfaction with life, happiness, positive outlook, and higher morale, along with reduced likelihood of depression. The positive impact of religious involvement on mental health was seen to be more robust among those under stressful circumstances such as persons with a disability or medical illness.

In a study involving 838 hospitalized older patients, the religious activities, attitudes, and spiritual experiences of the patients were associated with better psychological health, cognitive functioning, physical functioning, less severe illness, and greater social support. The social support enables one to be more resilient in adversity and better cope with life's problems.

With all of these health benefits it should come as no surprise that those who frequently attend religious services (at least once a week) have a 20-30 percent reduced likelihood of dying over a 30 year period. Overall, those who regularly attend church live 7 to 8 years longer than those who never attend. It was reported that African-Americans who attend religious services more than once a week live 14 years longer than those who did not attend church.

Religion may be an important way for people to cope with stress, and thereby ameliorate the negative effects of stress on their immune system. What people think and believe truly impacts their immune system. Recently, Dr Koenig found that men and women who regularly attended religious services were only one-half as likely to have elevated interleukin-6 levels (an indicator of a compromised immune system), than those who were less involved. Research conducted at Stanford University also found that religious involvement was positively associated with numbers of white blood cells and natural killer cells in the body. Scientists are discovering that what people think, believe, and feel may have a direct impact on neuroendocrine and immune function. These two systems play an important role in fighting disease and speeding recovery from illness.

In a 16-year study comparing the survival of 4,000 Israeli inhabitants who were members of either religious kibbutzim (communal settlement) or matched secular kibbutzim, it was found that the likelihood of dying was almost twice the level among the members of the secular communities compared to that of the religious communities.

Religious beliefs often provide an optimism that imbues traumatic life events with real purpose and meaning. Regular attendance at a church, synagogue or mosque also appears to be therapeutic for your health. According to Dr. Benson, worship services are full of potentially therapeutic elements such as music, prayer and contemplation, familiar rituals, distraction from everyday tensions, fellowship, and useful education classes. Religion appears to be more closely related to health than many people realize.

Visit **www.kyleeskitchen.com/simplyfresh/nutrition** to read more on the health and nutrition topics found here, plus bonus material found only on the website!

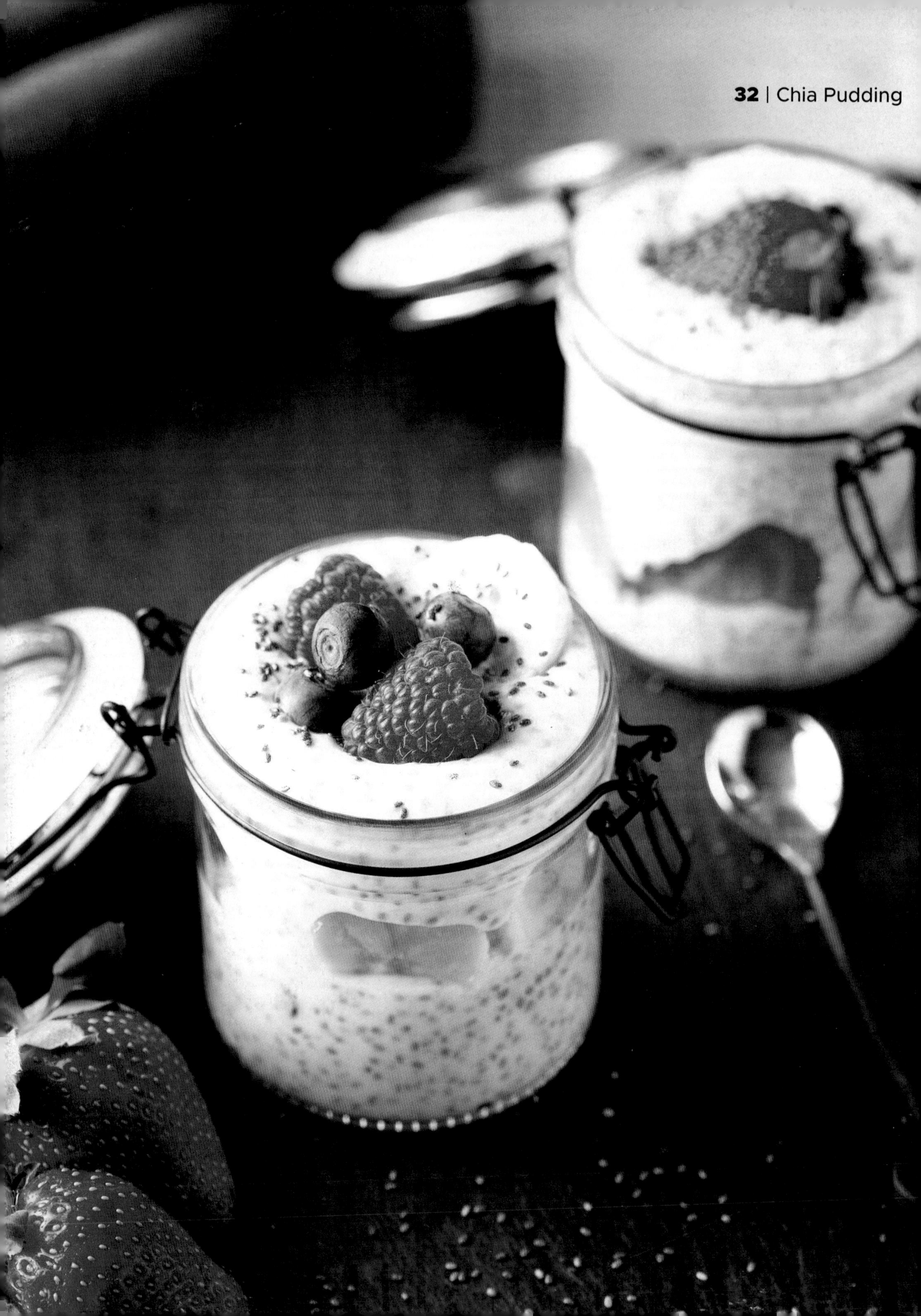

Breakfast

Pancakes

Prep	5 minutes
Cook	8-12 minutes
Makes	12 servings

Note: *To make this recipe soy-free, choose a non-dairy milk with no soy. To make it nut-free, use rice milk. Add fresh or frozen fruit to the pancake batter to mix things up. Slice up a banana and add a tablespoon or two of coconut flakes to the batter to make some Hawaiian pancakes.*

INGREDIENTS

1 c. whole wheat pastry flour

1 c. all-purpose flour

¼ t. salt

2 c. dairy-free milk

2 T. maple syrup

2 T. aluminum-free baking powder

Directions

In a large bowl, whisk together flour, baking powder, and salt. Add the dairy-free milk and maple syrup, stir until mixed well. Do not overtax the batter. For thinner pancakes, add more milk.

Over medium heat, place a pan and lightly oil. When small bubbles appear in the center of the pancake, then it's time to flip it. When the other side is golden brown then it's time to serve.

Nutrition Facts

Serving Size	1 pancake	Sodium	101mg
Calories	100	Carbs	20g
Fat	<1g	Fiber	1g
Sat. Fat	0g	Sugar	3g
Cholesterol	0g	Protein	3g

Waffles

Prep 8 minutes

Cook 5-10 minutes

Makes 12 servings

(NF) (SF) (D)

Note: *To make this recipe soy-free, choose a dairy-free milk with no soy. To make it nut-free, use rice milk. To avoid lumps in the batter, sift the flours through a fine sifter.*

INGREDIENTS

1 c. all-purpose flour

1 c. whole wheat flour

½ t. baking soda

1 t. aluminum-free baking powder

½ t. salt

3 T. organic sugar

3 T. ground flax seed, mixed with 9 T. water

2 T. dairy-free butter

2 c. dairy-free milk

Directions

Whisk the flours, baking powder, baking soda, salt and sugar in a medium bowl. Add the melted dairy-free butter, flaxseed and water combination and dairy-free milk, then stir until combined. Ladle the amount of waffle batter to cover all the holes of the waffle iron, and cook until the waffle is golden or until the waffle iron says it's done. Serve immediately, or keep warm in a 200° oven.

Nutrition Facts

Serving Size	1 square	Sodium	210mg
Calories	129	Carbs	21 g
Fat	4 g	Fiber	2 g
Sat. Fat	0 g	Sugar	5 g
Cholesterol	0 g	Protein	4 g

Biscuits & Gravy

Prep 10 minutes for each

Cook 15 minutes for biscuits, 7-10 minutes for gravy

Makes 12 biscuits, 16 servings of gravy

Note: If you are only going to need half of the amount of gravy, make the entire batch, and only heat half of it in the pan, and save the other half to use later in the week. It might sound strange, but try adding 1 cup frozen peas and eating it over toast or biscuits. It's a great way to get an extra serving of vegetables in with great flavor.

BISCUITS

1 c. all-purpose flour

1 c. whole wheat flour

1 T. aluminum-free baking powder

¾ t. salt

½ c. dairy-free butter, cold

¾ c. dairy-free milk

GRAVY

1 c. raw cashews

3½ c. water

½ t. salt

2 t. onion powder

½ t. garlic powder

1 T. McKay's chicken seasoning or other vegan imitation chicken seasoning

2 T. nutritional yeast flakes

3 T. flour

For the Biscuits

Preheat oven to 375˚. In a bowl, whisk together flour, baking powder and salt. Add the dairy-free butter, cutting it into the flour mixture by using a fork or a pastry cutter until the texture resembles a coarse meal. Add dairy-free milk and stir with a spoon until it is just combined.

On a lightly floured surface, transfer the dough and pat until it is about an inch thick. Using a cookie cutter or biscuit cutter, cut the biscuits out. Place them on a baking sheet that is lined with parchment paper or on a silicone mat. Bake for 12-15 minutes, or until they start to turn golden brown. Remove biscuits from the oven and transfer to a wire rack to cool.

For the Gravy

Place cashews and 1 cup of water into blender and blend on high for 2-3 minutes, or until smooth. Add the rest of the ingredients and water to the blender and blend for another 2-3 minutes.

Place into a pan and bring to a boil on a medium-high heat, stirring constantly to keep it from lumping or burning. Once it comes to a boil, continue stirring for another minute as it thickens, then remove from heat.

Nutrition Facts | Biscuits

Serving Size	1 biscuit	Sodium	275mg
Calories	109	Carbs	16 g
Fat	4 g	Fiber	1.4 g
Sat. Fat	<1 g	Sugar	<1 g
Cholesterol	0 g	Protein	2.8 g

Nutrition Facts | Gravy

Serving Size	¼ cup	Sodium	75mg
Calories	59	Carbs	4g
Fat	4g	Fiber	0.75g
Sat. Fat	<1g	Sugar	<1g
Cholesterol	0g	Protein	2g

Tofu Bacon

Prep 5 minutes

Cook 10 minutes

Makes 15 servings

(GF) (NF) (D)

Note: Use a gluten-free soy sauce option, such as Bragg's Liquid Aminos (see glossary) to make this recipe completely gluten-free. For a stronger smoke flavor add liquid smoke to taste. The tofu cooks best when using a little bit of oil or oil spray in the pan.

INGREDIENTS

Firm tofu, sliced

2 t. soy sauce

¼ c. nutritional yeast flakes

1 t. liquid smoke

½ t. smoked or mild paprika (this adds a little red coloring)

1-2 t. olive oil or vegetable spray

Directions

Heat oil over medium heat in a large non-stick skillet. Slice tofu into thin slices, and place them into your pan. Cook until nice and crispy brown. Usually I let them cook for 7-10 minutes on each side. Then season them. First add the soy sauce, nutritional yeast, paprika (if desired), and finally the liquid smoke. Sauté for one more minute, remove from heat, and enjoy.

Nutrition Facts

Serving Size	1 slice	Sodium	33mg
Calories	35	Carbs	2g
Fat	2g	Fiber	1g
Sat. Fat	0g	Sugar	0g
Cholesterol	0g	Protein	4g

Scrambled Tofu Tacos

Prep 10 minutes

Cook 7 minutes

Makes 7 servings

INGREDIENTS

14 oz. firm or extra firm tofu

1 t. salt

1 t. onion powder

1 t. garlic powder

2 t. McKay's chicken seasoning

¼ t. turmeric

¼ c. salsa

2 oz. veggie meat (optional)

tortillas

Directions

First, drain water from the tofu, and press out a lot of the retained water. Turn your burner on medium heat. Take the tofu into your hand and squeeze it through, until it crumbles into small pieces. Add salt, onion powder, garlic powder, chicken seasoning, and turmeric. Cook for 5-7 minutes, or until nice and hot, then stir in the salsa. Remove pan from heat and serve.

You can eat the scrambled tofu as is, or make breakfast tacos or burritos. Place tofu on tortilla, top with fresh diced tomatoes, lettuce, avocado, and cilantro.

Nutrition Facts

Serving Size	¼ c	Cholesterol	0g	Sugar	<1g
Calories	103	Sodium	529mg	Protein	8g
Fat	5g	Carbs	8g		
Sat. Fat	1g	Fiber	2g		

French Toast & Strawberry Sauce

Prep 7-10 minutes

Cook 8-10 minutes

Makes 8 servings

(GF) (NF) (SF) (D)

Note: By using half a banana it helps to give the french toast a nice texture, without a strong banana flavor. Use an unspotted banana for a milder flavor. Add a whole banana for a stronger banana flavor. Any type of fresh or frozen fruit can be used to make the fruit sauce. To make completely gluten-free, use a gluten-free bread.

FRENCH TOAST

1 lg. baguette or other vegan loaf, sliced diagonally

1 c. dairy-free milk

½ ripe banana

2 T. ground flax seed

½ t. vanilla extract

½ t. cinnamon

1-2 t. olive oil or vegetable spray

STRAWBERRY SAUCE

2 c. strawberries, trimmed and chopped

2 T. lemon juice, freshly squeezed

1 T. sugar

For the French Toast

In a blender, combine dairy-free milk, banana, ground flax seed, vanilla extract and cinnamon. Blend until completely smooth, approximately 2-3 minutes. Pour mixture into a shallow dish. Heat oil over medium-high heat in a large non-stick skillet. Dip each piece of bread into mixture then fry until it becomes golden brown. Flip and cook for an additional minute or so.

*Note: Some pans may need additional oil/spray when flipping to the other side.

For the Strawberry Sauce

In a small saucepan, combine all ingredients. Simmer over medium heat about 10 minutes or until the strawberries begin to break down. Pour over French toast.

Nutrition Facts

Serving Size	1 slice	Sodium	83mg
Calories	96	Carbs	14g
Fat	4g	Fiber	2.5g
Sat. Fat	1g	Sugar	2.6g
Cholesterol	0g	Protein	2.6g

Overnight Muesli

Prep	10 minutes
Total	4+ hours
Makes	4 servings

(GF) (SF) (D)

Note: To make this recipe soy-free, choose a non-dairy milk with no soy. To make it gluten-free, use gluten-free oats.

INGREDIENTS

1 c. oats

½ c. coconut milk

½ c. 100% pineapple juice

1 c. dairy-free milk

2 T. agave nectar

pinch of salt

1-2 oz. nuts

½ apple, chopped

½ c. pineapple, chopped

bunch grapes, sliced in half

1 banana, sliced

Directions

Add all ingredients in one bowl and mix well. Cover and place in fridge overnight or for a few hours until chilled. Serve next day.

Nutrition Facts

Serving Size	½ c	Sodium	37mg
Calories	340	Carbs	50g
Fat	14g	Fiber	5g
Sat. Fat	7g	Sugar	22g
Cholesterol	0g	Protein	7g

Pumpkin Pie Oatmeal

Prep 5 minutes
Cook 8-10 minutes
Makes 2 servings

(GF) (D)

INGREDIENTS

½ c. quick oats
1 c. water
pinch of salt
2 T. ground flaxseed
¼ t. pumpkin spice
¼ c. dairy-free milk

1½ T. pure maple syrup or agave nectar
¼ c. berries
1 oz. nuts

Directions

In small pot, add water and oats, place on medium-high heat. Stir occasionally as it comes to a boil. Allow it to boil for 1-2 minutes, or until it is desired consistency. Add sweetener, salt, pumpkin spice and flaxseed, then stir. Then add the remaining ingredients.

Nutrition Facts

Serving Size	1 c	Sodium	23mg
Calories	289	Carbs	33g
Fat	15.5g	Fiber	6.5g
Sat. Fat	1.5g	Sugar	13.5g
Cholesterol	0g	Protein	7.5g

Crockpot Oats

Prep 5 minutes
Cook 6+ hours
Makes 4 servings

(GF) (NF) (SF) (D)

INGREDIENTS

1 c. whole grain oats
2 c. water
1 c. dairy-free milk
⅛ t. salt
⅛-¼ c. fresh or dried fruit
2 T. pure maple syrup

Directions

Place oats, water, and salt in a crockpot on low and cook overnight. Serve with fresh or dried fruit. Add fruit once you are ready to eat, because dried fruit tends to swell when cooking. Add maple syrup, agave or honey to sweeten if needed.

Nutrition Facts

Serving Size	½ c	Sodium	80mg
Calories	129	Carbs	25g
Fat	2g	Fiber	2.5g
Sat. Fat	0g	Sugar	11g
Cholesterol	0g	Protein	3g

Chia Pudding

Prep	5 minutes
Total	1+ hours
Makes	5 servings

(GF) (NF) (SF) (D)

Note: To make this recipe soy-free, choose a non-dairy milk with no soy. To make it nut-free, use rice milk. Chia seeds are a great source of Omega-3 fatty acids and fiber. One ounce of chia seeds contains 11 grams of fiber, making these a great way to boost your fiber intake.

INGREDIENTS

1 c. dairy-free milk

1 c. dairy-free yogurt

2 T. pure maple syrup

1 t. vanilla extract

¼ c. chia seeds

1 c. fresh fruit

¼ c. sliced almonds

Directions

In a medium bowl, whisk milk and yogurt. Add maple syrup, vanilla and chia seeds. Stir until just blended. Place in fridge for at least one hour. Stir once more then top with fresh fruit and almonds. Serve chilled.

Nutrition Facts

Serving Size	½ c	Sodium	53mg
Calories	157	Carbs	16g
Fat	8.6g	Fiber	5.4g
Sat. Fat	<1g	Sugar	9g
Cholesterol	0g	Protein	5g

Lemon Poppy Seed Muffins

Prep 15 minutes

Bake 25 minutes

Makes 12 muffins

INGREDIENTS

2 c. whole wheat pastry flour
½ c. sugar
1½ T. poppy seeds
1 T. baking powder
½ t. salt
1 c. dairy-free milk
⅓ c. unsweetened applesauce
¼ c. fresh lemon juice
2 T. lemon zest
2 t. vanilla extract

Nutrition Facts

Serving Size	1	Sodium	132mg
Calories	152	Carbs	33g
Fat	1g	Fiber	2.5g
Sat. Fat	0g	Sugar	18g
Cholesterol	0g	Protein	3.4g

Directions for Muffins

Preheat oven to 375˚. Mix dry ingredients in a large bowl. Make a well in the center of the dry ingredients and add wet ingredients, then mix until just combined. Be careful to not over-mix the batter.

Coat muffin tins with non-stick cooking spray or use muffin liners. Fill each muffin cup ¾ of the way. Bake 22-25 minutes, or until a toothpick comes out clean. Transfer to a wire rack to cool completely.

Directions for Glaze

Mix ⅔ c. powdered sugar and 1 tablespoon of fresh lemon juice together in small bowl. Either use a spoon to drizzle glaze on each muffin, or dip top of each muffin into glaze. Excess may be stored in a sealed container for 3-4 days.

Sides

Garlic Green Beans

Prep 5 minutes

Cook 15 minutes

Makes 4 servings

(GF) (NF) (SF) (D)

Note: If you are in a hurry and do not have time to chop fresh garlic, simply use 1-2 teaspoons garlic powder. Replacing the green beans with asparagus or other vegetables is a great way to mix things up. If you don't steam the green beans before grilling, cover them while on the grill and add a few minutes to the cooking time.

INGREDIENTS

12 oz. fresh green beans

5-7 cloves garlic, minced

1 T. olive oil

salt to taste

Directions

Steam green beans for 3-5 minutes. On a grill, add about 1 tablespoons of olive oil, and place the steamed beans on the grill. Grill for about 5 minutes, then add minced garlic, continue grilling for another 5 minutes. Place green beans on serving plate, add salt to taste.

Nutrition Facts

Serving Size	3 oz	Sodium	1mg
Calories	55	Carbs	5.5g
Fat	3.5g	Fiber	2g
Sat. Fat	<1g	Sugar	0g
Cholesterol	0g	Protein	1g

Green Bean Casserole

(NF) (D) (SF) (hand)

INGREDIENTS

1 lb. green beans, cut in half, rinsed and trimmed
1 c. chopped mushrooms
¾ c. vegetable broth
1 c. unsweetened non-dairy milk
2 T. olive oil
½ med. onion, diced
2 T. flour
2 cloves garlic, minced
1 c. crispy fried onions
salt to taste

Directions (10 min prep, 35-45 min cook)

Preheat oven to 400°. In large pot, bring water to a boil. Add beans, cook for 5 min. Remove beans and cool immediately in ice water. Drain and put into a 9x13 baking dish. Place a large pot on medium heat. Add olive oil, garlic, and onion. Sauté until onions are transparent. Add mushrooms and salt to taste. Cook for another 2-3 minutes.

Whisk in flour and coat the veggies. Cook for one minute. Add vegetable broth slowly while whisking. add milk with a whisk. Cook for 5-7 min. until thick and bubbly. Taste to see if you need more salt.

Remove from heat and pour over green beans. Stir if needed. Place fried onions on top of casserole. Bake for 15-20 min. or until slightly golden brown. Serves 10.

Seasoned Popcorn

(GF) (NF) (SF) (D)

INGREDIENTS

½ c. popcorn kernels
½ t. onion powder
¼ t. garlic powder
¼ c. yeast flakes
3 T. olive oil
1½ T. water
½ t. dill weed
½ t. salt

Directions (5 min prep, 5 min cook)

Pop the popcorn in an air popper. In a separate bowl, add the remaining dry ingredients and stir. Add olive oil and stir until well combined. Place popcorn in large bowl with lid, this will make it easier to coat popcorn. Pour topping mix onto popcorn, close lid and shake it until popcorn is well coated. Add more oil if needed. Serves 8.

Nutrition Facts | Popcorn

Serving Size	1 c	Sodium	143mg
Calories	56	Carbs	5g
Fat	4g	Fiber	1g
Sat. Fat	<1g	Sugar	0g
Cholesterol	0g	Protein	2g

Nutrition Facts | Green Bean Casserole

Serving Size	3 oz	Sodium	72mg
Calories	87	Carbs	5g
Fat	7g	Fiber	1g
Sat. Fat	0.9g	Sugar	2g
Cholesterol	0g	Protein	1g

Tofu Ricotta Cheese

(GF) (NF) (D)

INGREDIENTS

14 oz. extra-firm tofu
8 oz. spinach, frozen, drained and thawed
½ t. garlic powder
1 t. onion powder
1 t. salt
2 T. nutritional yeast flakes
¼ c. sour cream of choice (p.106)

Directions (15-20 min prep)

Drain excess water from tofu. Pat with paper towels if needed, or allow to drain in a colander for 15 minutes.
In a medium bowl, mash the tofu with hands or use a potato masher. Add remaining ingredients to tofu and mix until well combined.

This can be used in making lasagna, stuffed shells, manicotti, or other desired dishes. Serves 9.

Nutrition Facts

Serving Size	¼ c	Sodium	273mg
Calories	64	Carbs	3g
Fat	4g	Fiber	1g
Sat. Fat	1g	Sugar	0g
Cholesterol	0g	Protein	8g

Brazilian Black Beans

(GF) (NF) (SF) (D)

INGREDIENTS

2 c. black beans, rinsed and soaked 2+ hrs.
8-10 c. water, added over time
4-7 cloves garlic, minced
½ onion, minced
2-3 T. olive oil
3 bay leaves
salt to taste

Directions (2+ hrs prep, 2-3 hrs cook)

Place olive oil, garlic, and onion into a large pot on medium-high heat. Sauté until onions are transparent. Add 4 cups of water, black beans, salt and bay leaves. Allow beans to cook until they are soft and tender. It usually takes between 2-3 hours to fully cook.
Continue to add water throughout the cooking time, checking periodically to ensure they don't lose too much water.

Nutrition Facts

Serving Size	½ c	Sodium	69mg
Calories	69	Carbs	7g
Fat	3.5g	Fiber	2.4g
Sat. Fat	<1g	Sugar	<1g
Cholesterol	0g	Protein	2.4g

Corn Bread Muffins

Prep	10 minutes
Bake	20 minutes
Makes	18-20 muffins

INGREDIENTS

- 2 T. ground flax seed with 6 T. water
- ⅓ c. maple syrup, agave or honey
- 1½ c. whole wheat pastry flour
- ⅓ c. turbinado sugar
- 3 T. dairy-free butter, melted
- ½ c. dairy-free milk
- ¾ c. creamed corn
- ½ t. salt
- ⅓ c. canola oil
- ½ c. corn meal
- 1 T. baking powder

Directions

Preheat oven to 350°. Line muffin tins with 18-20 paper cups.

In medium bowl, combine dry ingredients. In a separate bowl, combine dairy-free milk, sweetener of choice, oil, flaxseed mixture and butter. Add to the dry ingredients and stir until just blended. Pour into muffin cups by filling ⅔ full. Bake for 18-20 minutes or until golden brown. Test with a toothpick inserted into center of muffin. Remove and let it set for 2-3 minutes, then place on a wire rack to cool for a few minutes. Serve warm.

Corn Bread: Pour batter into greased 8 inch baking pan. Bake 35 minutes or until toothpick comes out clean.

Nutrition Facts

Serving Size	1 muffin		
Calories	107	Sodium	103mg
Fat	5g	Carbs	15g
Sat. Fat	<1g	Fiber	1.4g
Cholesterol	0g	Sugar	6g
		Protein	2g

Brown Rice

Prep 3 minutes
Cook 30-35 minutes
Makes 4 servings

(GF) (NF) (SF) (D)

INGREDIENTS

1 c. brown rice,
   rinsed and drained

2 c. water

½-1 t. salt

1-2 T. olive oil

Directions

In a pot, add olive oil and rice, on a medium heat. Sauté the rice until it is a little bit golden brown and somewhat dry. Add water and bring to a boil. Once it begins boiling, add salt, boil for 3-4 more minutes. Put the lid on the pot, turn heat to low. Allow rice to cook for 30-35 minutes, until the water has evaporated and the rice is tender.

Nutrition Facts

Serving Size	½ c	Sodium	587mg
Calories	159	Carbs	27g
Fat	4.5g	Fiber	2g
Sat. Fat	<1g	Sugar	0.5g
Cholesterol	0g	Protein	3g

Quinoa

Prep 3 minutes
Cook 20 minutes
Makes 6 servings

(GF) (NF) (SF) (D)

INGREDIENTS

1 c. quinoa

2 t. oil or water

1½ c water

½ t. salt

Directions

In medium saucepan, add quinoa and 2 teaspoons oil or water to sauté the quinoa. Over a medium heat, brown quinoa for 3-5 minutes or until golden brown, stirring frequently so it doesn't burn. Add the water and salt, then bring to a boil. Boil for one minute, then reduce the heat to low. Continue cooking for 10-15 minutes or until all the water is gone and absorbed into the quinoa. Remove from heat and serve.

Nutrition Facts

Serving Size	¼ c	Sodium	300mg
Calories	173	Carbs	27g
Fat	5g	Fiber	3.5g
Sat. Fat	<1g	Sugar	1g
Cholesterol	0g	Protein	5.5g

Salad

Corn & Edamame Salad

Prep 10 minutes

Makes 12 servings

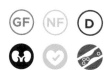

Note: If you do not have cilantro, try replacing it with green onions or parsley for a different flavor. A great way to give salad more flavor is by adding fresh lemon juice to it. It gives it a fresh, healthy kick.

INGREDIENTS

5 ears of corn, boiled or roasted

1 ½ c. edamame, frozen

2 tomatoes, sliced

3 T. green onion, chopped

2 T. cilantro, chopped

juice of one lemon

salt to taste

Directions

Cut kernels off the cob, then place in a bowl. Put the edamame in a small pot with enough water to cover, boil for 2-3 minutes. Drain and mix with corn and the other ingredients, stirring until well mixed. Chill thoroughly in fridge, then serve.

Nutrition Facts

Serving Size	½ c	Sodium	0mg
Calories	51	Carbs	8g
Fat	1.4g	Fiber	2g
Sat. Fat	0g	Sugar	2g
Cholesterol	0g	Protein	3g

Southwestern Salad

Prep 15 minutes

Makes 14 servings

(GF) (NF) (SF) (D)

Note: Feel free to add or take away ingredients to make it your own. Try kidney beans, purple onions, red bell pepper, or whatever tickles your fancy. This salad goes great with the Cilantro Dressing on page 105.

INGREDIENTS

1 large head of romaine lettuce

15 oz. can black beans, rinsed and drained

1 lg. orange bell pepper

5 green onions

1 pint cherry tomatoes

1 large avocado

2 c. corn (fresh or frozen, thawed)

½ c. heart of palm, sliced (optional)

Directions

Finely chop romaine, bell pepper, tomatoes, and green onions. Place all ingredients in a large bowl and toss. Toss in dressing or serve it on the side.

Nutrition Facts

Serving Size	½ c	Sodium	75mg
Calories	99	Carbs	18g
Fat	2g	Fiber	6g
Sat. Fat	0g	Sugar	3g
Cholesterol	0g	Protein	5g

Super Kale Salad

Prep 10 minutes

Makes 8 servings

Note: By massaging the kale with your hands, you tenderize it so it's not as tough. If you are not into massaging your kale, then simply add the dressing to the kale and let it sit in the refrigerator overnight to help tenderize it.

SALAD

4 c. finely chopped kale, ribs removed

15 oz. can chickpeas, rinsed and drained

⅔ c. dried cranberries

1 c. edamame beans, cooked and cooled

½ c. carrot shreds

Garnish with cherry tomatoes

DRESSING

3 T. lemon juice

4 T. extra virgin olive oil

¾ t. dried Italian herb blend

¼ t. kosher salt

Add all dressing ingredients to a large salad bowl and whisk until combined.

Place kale, chickpeas, cranberries, shredded carrots, and edamame into a large bowl.

Add dressing to the salad and mix well.

Nutrition Facts

Serving Size	1 c	Sodium	180mg
Calories	197	Carbs	24g
Fat	9g	Fiber	6g
Sat. Fat	1g	Sugar	8g
Cholesterol	0g	Protein	7g

Brazilian Potato Salad

Prep   10 minutes

Cook   10 minutes

Makes   8 servings

Note: *If you are wanting a more traditional potato salad, replace the olives, peas and corn with green onions and paprika.*

INGREDIENTS

1 lb. potatoes of choice

1 c. vegan mayonnaise

½ c. corn kernels

½ c. peas

½ t. salt

8-10 green olives, sliced

Directions

Dice potatoes into pieces about ¼ inch, or bite size. Boil for about 7-10 minutes, until the potatoes are tender when pierced with a fork or knife. Drain the potatoes in a colander, then place into a bowl. Add 1 cup of vegan mayonnaise then smash them until the texture is mashed potatoes and potato salad. Add peas, corn, salt and green olives, then stir until it is all mixed well. Place in fridge and chill for at least one hour. If you use frozen peas and carrots the cooling process will take less time. Serve when chilled.

Nutrition Facts

Serving Size	½ c	Sodium	374mg
Calories	178	Carbs	28g
Fat	6.5g	Fiber	3.4g
Sat. Fat	1g	Sugar	3.6g
Cholesterol	0g	Protein	3.3g

Black Bean Salad

Prep   10 minutes

Makes   16 servings

INGREDIENTS

2 cans (3 c.) black beans, rinsed

2 cans (3 c.) corn, rinsed

1 c. edamame

2 tomatoes, diced

2 avocados, diced

3-4 T. cilantro, heaping

4 T. lemon juice

salt to taste

Directions

In a bowl, combine drained black beans, corn, edamame, cilantro, lemon juice and salt. Stir until it is well combined. Gently stir in the diced tomatoes and avocados.

Nutrition Facts

Serving Size	½ c	Sodium	110mg
Calories	148	Carbs	24g
Fat	3.8g	Fiber	7g
Sat. Fat	<1g	Sugar	2.6g
Cholesterol	0g	Protein	7.3g

Fruit Salad

Prep   8 minutes

Makes   8 servings

(GF) (NF) (SF) (D)

Note: You can use any type of fresh fruit and add lime and fresh mint to give it extra flavor. The lime also helps to keep the fruit from browning, so it will stay good for a day or two after you make it.

INGREDIENTS

1 fresh pineapple, chopped

2 ripe mangoes, diced

1 c. fresh blueberries

2-3 T. fresh mint, chopped

juice of one lime

Directions

Chop pineapple and mangoes into bite size pieces, then add to a large bowl. Add the blueberries and chopped mint. Juice a fresh lime over the fruit and mix until all the fruit is covered and combined.

Nutrition Facts

Serving Size	1 c	Sodium	2mg
Calories	98	Carbs	25g
Fat	0g	Fiber	3g
Sat. Fat	0g	Sugar	20g
Cholesterol	0g	Protein	1g

Cucumber Dill Salad

Prep 5 minutes
Serves 3 servings

(GF) (NF) (SF) (D)

Note: Make this salad a few hours, or even the night before serving, that way the cucumbers will absorb the dressing, and give an even bolder flavor.

INGREDIENTS

2 medium cucumbers, thinly sliced

½ medium red onion, thinly sliced

2 T. fresh dill

2 T. fresh lemon juice

2 t. olive oil

½ t. salt

2 t. Dijon mustard

Directions

Begin by slicing cucumbers and onions thinly. Place into a serving bowl. In a small bowl, combine the remaining ingredients. Mix until well combined, then pour over the cucumbers and onions. Toss thoroughly, then serve.

Nutrition Facts

Serving Size	½ c	Sodium	31mg
Calories	52	Carbs	5g
Fat	3g	Fiber	1g
Sat. Fat	0g	Sugar	3g
Cholesterol	0g	Protein	1g

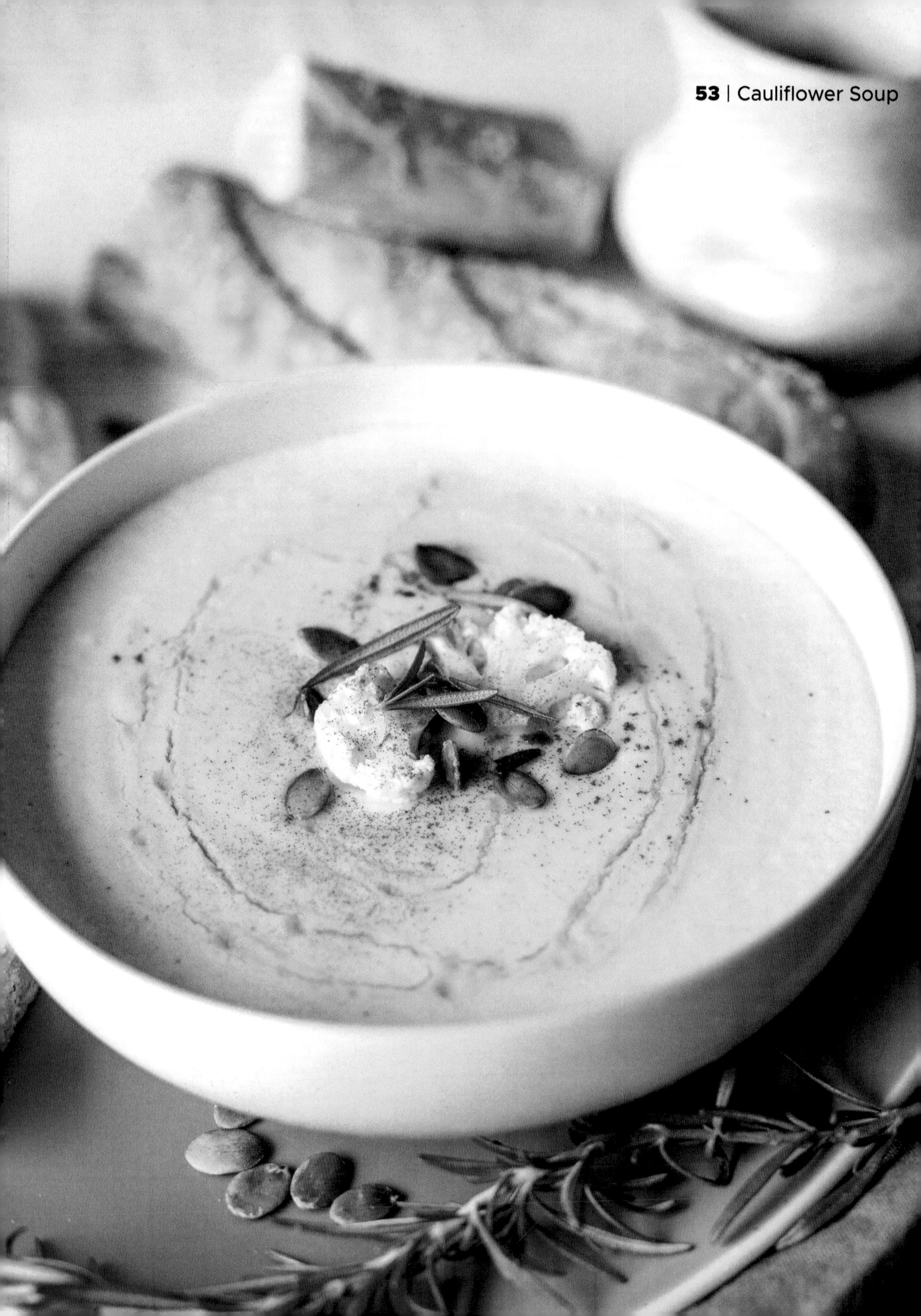

Soup

Red Lentil Soup

Prep	5 minutes
Cook	20-30 minutes
Makes	8 servings

GF NF SF D

Note: This recipe can be used with any type of lentil or other legume, however, cook time will vary.

INGREDIENTS

2 c. red lentils

4 c. water (more if needed)

2 T. garlic, minced

¼ c. onion, diced

2 T. olive oil

1½ t. salt

2 T. McKay's chicken seasoning

2 bay leaves

Dash of cayenne

1 T. nutritional yeast flakes

Directions

Turn burner on to medium-high. In a pot, add oil, onion and garlic. Sauté until onions are transparent. Add lentils and water into pot. After cooking about 3 minutes, add the remaining ingredients. Let the lentils cook for about 15 minutes, or until soft. More water may be needed. Remove frome heat and serve.

Nutrition Facts

Serving Size	½ c	Sodium	440mg
Calories	196	Carbs	29g
Fat	4g	Fiber	11g
Sat. Fat	<1g	Sugar	3g
Cholesterol	0g	Protein	13g

Cauliflower Soup

Prep 10 minutes

Cook 20 minutes

Serves 10 servings

INGREDIENTS

¾ c. cashews

4½ c. water

1 small onion, diced

6 c. cauliflower

3 T. McKay's chicken seasoning

salt to taste

Directions

Blend the cashews with 1 cup of water for 2-3 minutes. In a large pot, sauté the onion in a small amount of oil or water, until translucent. Add the cauliflower, seasonings and remaining water, then boil on medium-high for 7-10 minutes, or until cauliflower is soft. Place mixture into blender and blend until the consistency is smooth. Reheat in the pot for 3-5 minutes, then serve.

Nutrition Facts

Serving Size	1 c	Sodium	136mg
Calories	72	Carbs	6g
Fat	5g	Fiber	1.5g
Sat. Fat	1g	Sugar	1.6g
Cholesterol	0g	Protein	2.8g

Rosemary Potato Soup & Garlic Croutons

Prep 15 minutes

Cook 30 minutes

Makes 15 servings

(GF) (NF) (SF) (D)

Note: Garnish the soup with croutons and a fresh sprig of rosemary to give it an elegant finish. Use a gluten-free bread to make this recipe completely gluten-free.

ROSEMARY POTATO SOUP

2 T. olive oil

1 yellow onion, diced

1 lb. red potatoes, quartered

2 cloves garlic

5 c. vegetable stock

1 bunch fresh rosemary, tied up with butcher's twine

1 t. salt

GARLIC CROUTONS

1 small baguette, sliced and chopped (about 2 cups)

2 tbsp olive oil

1 garlic clove, minced

salt to taste

For the Soup

Place oil in the pot to heat. Add the onion and garlic. Sauté until tender, about 5 minutes. Then add potatoes and broth. Simmer, loosely covered, for 10 mins. Add rosemary and allow to simmer for 5 mins. Soup is done when potatoes are fork tender. Allow to cool slightly. Remove rosemary.

Meanwhile, make the croutons.

For the Croutons

Slice baguette into slices and then cut in bite-sized chunks. Toss with olive oil, garlic, salt and pepper. Bake at 375° for 5–10 mins until golden brown. Set aside to cool.

In a blender, puree soup in batches or with immersion blender. Portion into bowls and garnish with a drizzle of olive oil, freshly chopped rosemary and garlic croutons.

Nutrition Facts

Serving Size	½ c	Sodium	160mg
Calories	105	Carbs	15.5g
Fat	4g	Fiber	2.6g
Sat. Fat	<1g	Sugar	3g
Cholesterol	0g	Protein	3g

Vegetable Soup

Prep 15 minutes
Cook 40 minutes
Makes 12 servings

(NF) (SF) (D)

INGREDIENTS

3 medium potatoes, diced ½" thick

2 t. McKay's chicken seasoning

4 carrots, peeled and chopped

1 c. whole wheat pasta shells

1 medium onion, chopped

2 stalks celery, chopped

1 bulb of garlic, minced

64 oz. vegetable broth

2-3 T. olive oil

1 c. green beans

3 tomatoes, diced

½ c. corn

½ c. peas

2 bay leaves

2 t. salt (to taste)

Directions

Over medium heat, in a large pot add the olive oil, onions, carrots and celery, then sauté for 3-4 minutes. Add the garlic and sauté for another minute. Add vegetable broth, tomatoes, potatoes, bay leaves, chicken seasoning and salt. Bring to a boil for 3 minutes, then add the green beans. Boil for another 20 minutes, then add pasta and boil an additional 10 minutes. Add corn and peas, then cook 5 more minutes. Serve warm.

Nutrition Facts

Serving Size	1 c	Sodium	881mg
Calories	142	Carbs	24g
Fat	4g	Fiber	4g
Sat. Fat	<1g	Sugar	4g
Cholesterol	0g	Protein	5g

Navy Bean Soup

Prep 4-8 hours

Cook 2+ hours

Makes 12 servings

(GF) (NF) (SF) (D)

INGREDIENTS

1 lb. navy or great northern beans

10-12 c. water

5 cloves garlic, minced

½ medium onion, diced

1 t. onion powder

1 t. garlic powder

1½ T. McKay's chicken seasoning (optional)

1 T. Bac'n bits (bacon-flavored vegetable protein), optional

1 t. salt

Directions

Soak beans 4-8 hours, then drain and add fresh water. Place beans in a crockpot on medium heat. The amount of water can vary, so start with about 10 cups then add more if needed. Add all of the ingredients to the crockpot, and allow to cook overnight, or 6-14 hours (until beans are soft).

For cooking on stovetop, place beans in a large pot with 12 cups of water, on medium-high heat. More water may be needed so keep an eye on them. Add the rest of the ingredients once the beans come to a boil. Boil beans for 3 or more hours until beans are soft and ready.

Nutrition Facts

Serving Size	½ c	Sodium	103mg
Calories	128	Carbs	23g
Fat	0g	Fiber	6g
Sat. Fat	0g	Sugar	0g
Cholesterol	0g	Protein	9g

Tomato Soup

Prep   20 minutes

Cook   1 hour 35 minutes

Makes   6-8 servings

(GF) (NF) (SF) (D)

Note: To make this recipe soy-free, choose a non-dairy milk with no soy. To make it nut-free, use rice milk. If you are wanting to cut down on bake and prep time, simply skip roasting the tomatoes. It will give it a different flavor, but it's still delicious.

INGREDIENTS

4 lbs. tomatoes, halved with seeds removed

5 T. olive oil

1 T. organic sugar

6 sprigs fresh thyme

1 medium onion, diced

4 cloves garlic, chopped

3 c. vegetable stock

1 bay leaf

½ c. dairy-free milk

3 T. fresh basil, chopped

salt to taste

Directions

Line a baking sheet with parchment paper or a silicone mat. Preheat oven to 400°. Halve and remove seeds from tomatoes, place cut-side up on baking sheet. Drizzle 3 tablespoons of olive oil over tomatoes, and sprinkle with about 1 teaspoon of salt and the sugar. Place the sprigs of thyme on the tomatoes. Roast for about one hour, or until they are wrinkly and soft. Let them cool before handling.

In a large pot, add 2 tablespoons of olive oil over a medium heat. Add the onions, a pinch of salt and the garlic, then cook until the onions are a light brown. Peel the skins off of the tomatoes and place them in the pot. Add the vegetable stock and bay leaf to the pot as well. Tie the thyme into a bundle with cooking string, and add to the pot. Partially cover the pot with a lid and cook for about 30 minutes. Turn the heat to low and add the dairy-free milk and basil, then simmer for 5 minutes. Remove bay leaf and thyme from the pot. You can either use a blender or immersion blender to puree the soup until it's smooth. Add salt to taste, about 2 teaspoons. Garnish with fresh basil leaves.

Nutrition Facts

Serving Size	1 c	Sodium	290mg
Calories	120	Carbs	9g
Fat	9g	Fiber	1g
Sat. Fat	1g	Sugar	7g
Cholesterol	0g	Protein	2g

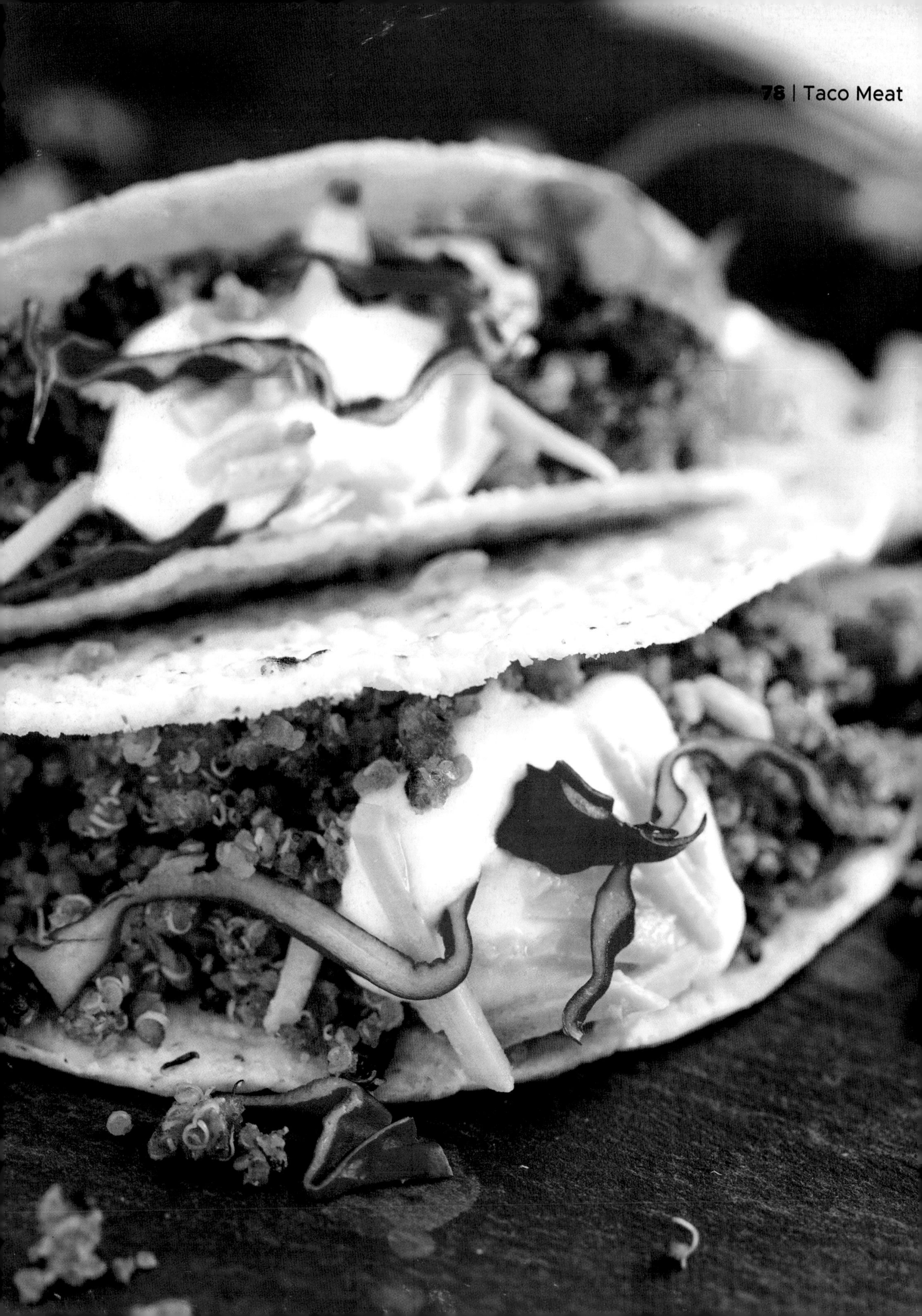

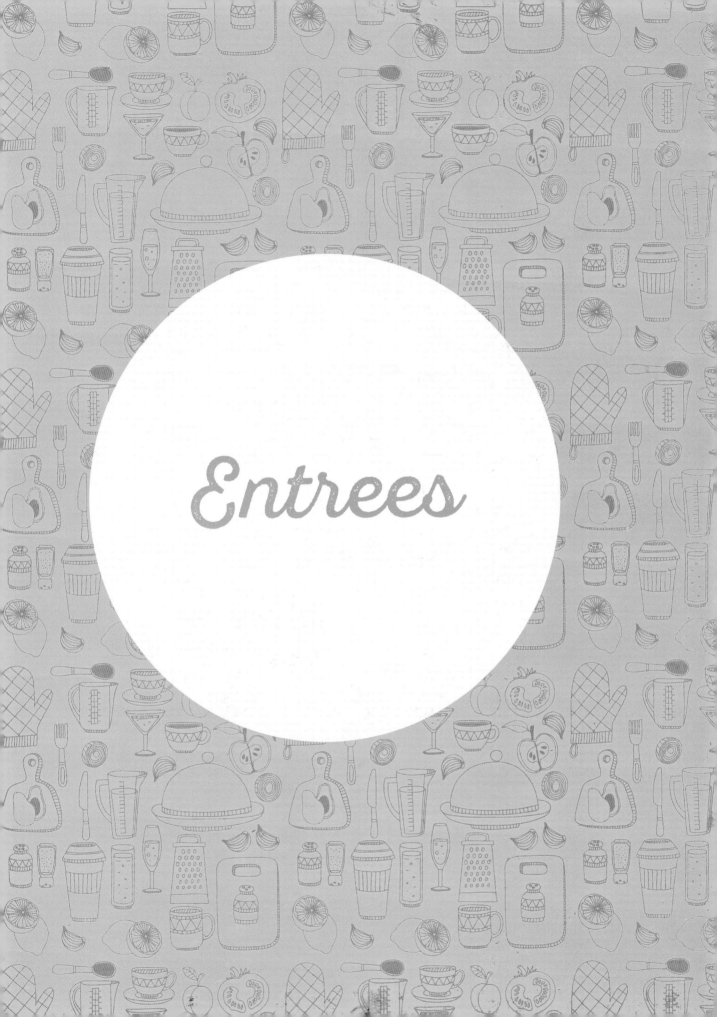

Entrees

Tofu Lettuce Wraps

Prep   15 minutes

Cook   15 minutes

Makes   12 servings

Note: Try the tofu over brown rice or quinoa for a different texture and meal, or add quinoa or brown rice to the lettuce wraps to add more fiber and substance. To make this recipe nut-free, do not use peanut sauce.

TOFU LETTUCE WRAPS

2 t. canola oil

1 T. sesame seed oil

1/4 c. onion, diced

3 green onions, sliced

3-5 cloves garlic, minced

1/2 c. carrots, shredded

8 oz. can water chestnuts, diced

14 oz. extra firm tofu, drained and diced small

2 T. soy sauce, low sodium

1 T. agave nectar or maple syrup

10-12 romaine lettuce leaves

PEANUT SAUCE

5 T. natural peanut butter

3 T. water

1 T. low-sodium soy sauce

4 T. fresh lime juice

2 t. agave, honey or maple syrup

2 cloves garlic

pinch of salt

For the Lettuce wraps

In a large frying pan, add canola oil, onions and garlic, sauté until onions are translucent. Add green onions, carrots, tofu, water chestnuts and sesame oil, then sauté for another 5-8 minutes. Stir in soy sauce and sweetener, cook 5 minutes. Remove from heat and allow to cool for 5 minutes before serving in the lettuce leaves. Drizzle peanut sauce on each lettuce wrap.

For the Peanut sauce

Place all ingredients into a blender and blend until it is smooth and creamy, about 3-5 minutes.

Nutrition Facts | Lettuce Wraps

Serving Size	¼ c	Sodium	106mg
Calories	67	Carbs	5g
Fat	4g	Fiber	1g
Sat. Fat	0g	Sugar	2g
Cholesterol	0g	Protein	4g

Nutrition Facts | Peanut Sauce

Serving Size	1 Tbsp	Sodium	63mg
Calories	36	Carbs	2g
Fat	2.5g	Fiber	0g
Sat. Fat	0g	Sugar	1g
Cholesterol	0g	Protein	1.5g

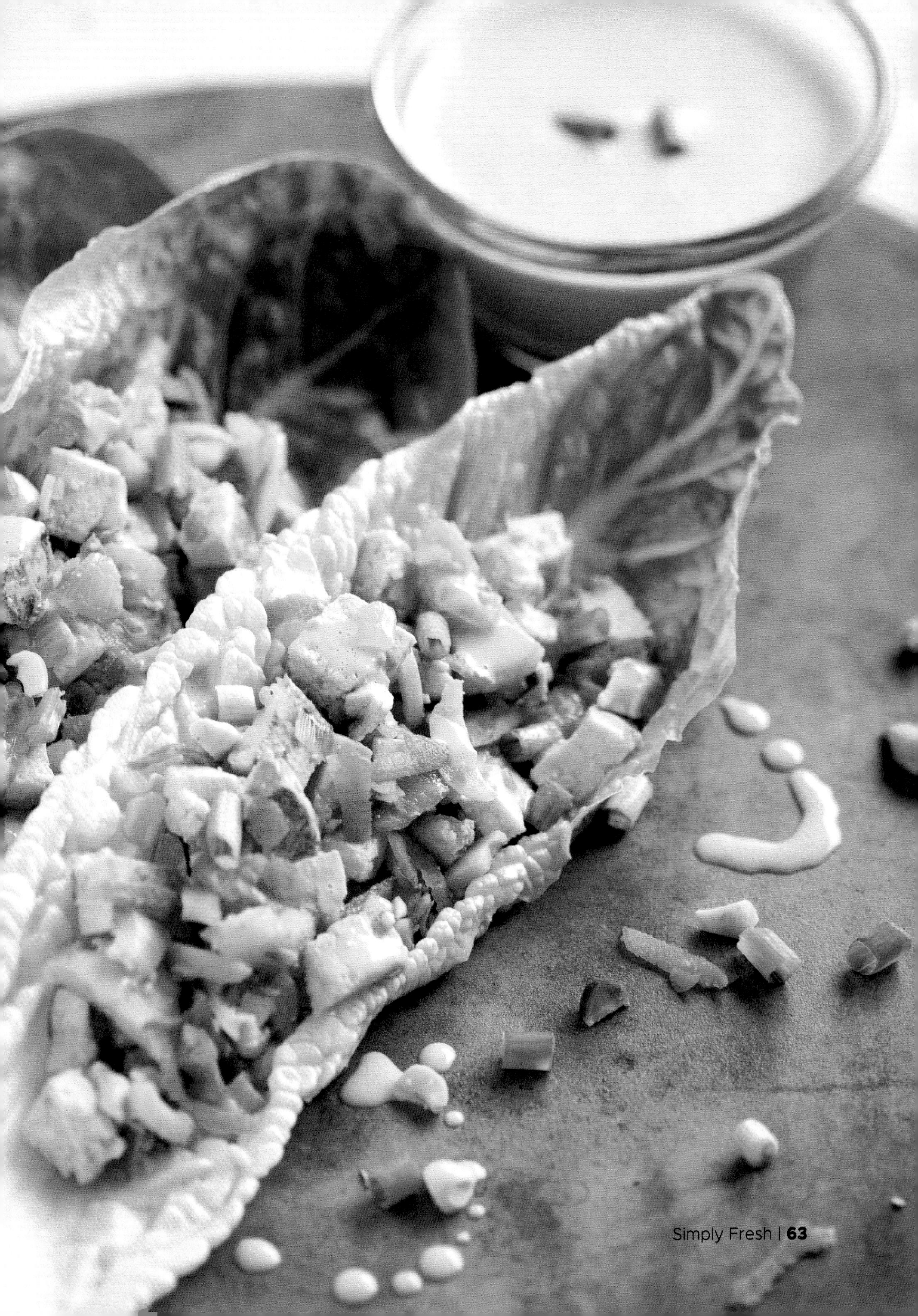

Crab Cakes

Prep   20 minutes
Bake   20-25 minutes
Makes   10 Servings

(NF) (SF) (D)

Note: *To make these extra crispy, dredge them an extra time.*

CRAB CAKES

2 c. marinated artichoke hearts

¼ c. green onions, chopped

½ c. celery, chopped

2 T. liquid from artichoke hearts

1 t. lemon juice

½ c. all-purpose or chickpea flour

2 t. sugar

1 t. Old Bay Seasoning

¼ t. salt

HORSERADISH TARTAR SAUCE

⅔ c. vegan mayonnaise

3 t. horseradish

1 T. lemon juice

1 T. fresh dill, finely chopped

For the crab cakes

Drain the marinated artichokes, reserving 2 tablespoons of the liquid to use in the recipe. Chop artichoke hearts into small pieces and add to a large mixing bowl with the remaining ingredients. Combine well using a fork or spoon.

Set up process line: Flour in a wide, shallow dish, breadcrumbs in another wide, shallow dish, and milk in a bowl.

Take a small handful of the artichoke mixture and form a round patty with your hands. Place "crab cake" in flour and coat all sides evenly. Submerge in milk, then remove and coat evenly with breadcrumbs. Repeat until all cakes are made.

Place patties onto a lined baking sheet. Bake at 350˚ for 20-25 minutes. Flip patties half way through baking.

For the horseradish tartar sauce

Place all ingredients into a bowl and stir until well mixed. Place in fridge until ready to serve.

Nutrition Facts | Crab Cakes

Serving Size	1 cake	Sodium	84mg
Calories	75	Carbs	10g
Fat	3g	Fiber	3.4g
Sat. Fat	0g	Sugar	<1g
Cholesterol	0g	Protein	2g

Nutrition Facts | Tartar Sauce

Serving Size	1 Tbsp	Sodium	122mg
Calories	5	Carbs	<1g
Fat	5g	Fiber	0g
Sat. Fat	<1g	Sugar	0g
Cholesterol	0g	Protein	0g

Eggless Salad Sandwich

Prep   10 minutes

Makes   6 servings

Note: One egg contains almost as much cholesterol as is recommended for the entire day. An egg sandwich can easily contain the maximum amount recommended for that day. By substituting this tofu salad for a regular egg salad sandwich, one can easily begin to lower their cholesterol and fat levels. Plus, you'll be saving plenty of calories!

INGREDIENTS

1 lb. extra firm tofu

¼ t. turmeric

2 T. nutritional yeast flakes

1 T. McKay's chicken seasoning

½ c. mayonnaise of choice

1 stalk celery, minced

2 green onions, finely chopped

salt to taste

Directions

Mash tofu in a small bowl, then add seasonings and stir well. Mix in green onions and celery, add salt to taste. Finally, add the mayonnaise.

Nutrition Facts

Serving Size	½ c	Sodium	365mg
Calories	150	Carbs	5g
Fat	11g	Fiber	2g
Sat. Fat	1g	Sugar	<1g
Cholesterol	0g	Protein	11g

Lemon Basil Pasta

Prep 10 minutes

Cook 10-15 minutes

Makes 8 servings

INGREDIENTS

⅔ c. extra virgin olive oil

⅔ c. nutritional yeast flakes

zest of one lemon

juice of two lemons

¼ - ½ c. chopped basil

1 pkg. whole wheat pasta of your choice

salt to taste (about 1 t.)

Note: *To make gluten-free, choose a gluten-free pasta*

Directions

Cook pasta according to directions. Meanwhile, mix the remaining ingredients together in a bowl. Before straining pasta, reserve about ¼ cup of the pasta water. Once the pasta is strained, add it to the bowl and stir until pasta is well covered with the mixture. You may want to add the pasta water to assist with texture.

Nutrition Facts

Serving Size	2 oz	Sodium	303mg
Calories	370	Carbs	50g
Fat	16g	Fiber	11g
Sat. Fat	2g	Sugar	1.6g
Cholesterol	0g	Protein	15g

Oat Burgers

Prep 25 minutes
Cook 30 minutes
Makes 24 servings

Note: To make this recipe gluten-free, use gluten-free oats and Bragg's Liquid Aminos in place of soy sauce. Make a batch or two of these burgers to enjoy them for the entire month. Freeze burgers by placing wax paper between the layers. They will keep for about 30 days frozen.

INGREDIENTS

5 c. water

1 ½ T. low-sodium soy sauce

½ c. olive oil

2 pkgs. onion soup mix (½ c. dry)

2 T. McKay's beef seasoning

1 medium onion, finely diced

⅛ t. cayenne pepper

1 t. poultry seasoning (blend of thyme, sage, marjoram, nutmeg and rosemary)

1 t. granulated garlic

4 c. old fashioned rolled oats

2 c. walnuts, finely diced or ground

2 T. sesame seeds

Directions

In large bowl, mix the oats, walnuts and sesame seeds. In a large pot mix water, soy sauce, oil, diced onion, broth seasoning, onion soup mix, cayenne pepper and chicken seasoning, then bring just to a boil. Reduce heat to low for 3 minutes, then turn off. Add oat mixture, mix briefly, then cover and let stand for 10 minutes. Mix again, briefly, then let it cool for 20 minutes, or until cool to touch.

Make each patty with ½ cup of mixture. Bake at 375° for 15 minutes, then flip and bake another 15 minutes (or until golden). Use parchment paper or a silicon mat on your baking sheet to prevent sticking. Let sit for 5 minutes before placing on a cooling rack. Serve warm.

Nutrition Facts

Serving Size	**1 burger**	Sodium	237mg
Calories	169	Carbs	12g
Fat	12g	Fiber	2g
Sat. Fat	1.5g	Sugar	<1g
Cholesterol	0g	Protein	4g

Turkey Loaf

Prep 25 minutes

Cook 1 hour 15 minutes

Makes 20 servings

Note: This is a great entree to use for the holidays in place of turkey. For leftovers try slicing it thinly and making a sandwich. It turns out delicious! To make this loaf soy-free, use Bragg's Liquid Aminos in place of soy sauce.

INGREDIENTS

2 ½ c. vital gluten flour

½ c. nutritional yeast flakes

1 t. thyme

½ t. rubbed sage

1 t. onion powder

1 t. salt

2 t. McKay's chicken seasoning (optional)

2 c. vegetable broth

¼ c. olive oil

1 T. Soy sauce

Puff Pastry (vegan)

Directions

In a mixing bowl, combine all dry ingredients. In another bowl, mix all wet ingredients. Combine both dry and wet ingredients with a spoon, or your hand, until it is mixed well. Form into a loaf with your hands. Unwrap cheese cloth, then place the loaf onto it. Roll up cheese cloth and place string on the ends to hold loaf.

Get a pot of water boiling (enough to cover loaf). Place loaf into boiling water, then reduce heat to medium-high. Continually check to ensure loaf is covered. Leave in water for 50-60 minutes. Remove loaf with tongs. Allow it to cool, then remove cheese cloth.

You can serve the loaf like this or add puff pastry to the outside to make it look more like a turkey. Roll out puff pastry and wrap the loaf in it. Brush olive oil on the top to help brown. Place loaf in the oven at 400° for 20-25 minutes, or until golden brown.

Nutrition Facts

Serving Size	1 slice	Sodium	160mg
Calories	62	Carbs	5g
Fat	1g	Fiber	1g
Sat. Fat	0g	Sugar	0g
Cholesterol	0g	Protein	8.3g

Tuna Salad

Prep   8 minutes

Makes   10 servings

(GF) (NF) (SF) (D)

Note: *To make this recipe soy-free, choose a mayonnaise that does not contain soy, like the recipe found on page 103. The Old Bay Seasoning is what helps to give it the "seafood" flavor, so don't skip out on this ingredient. If you are in a rush to pack a lunch, this is always a great go-to recipe.*

INGREDIENTS

15 oz. can chickpeas, drained

¼ c. vegan mayonnaise

2 stalks celery, finely chopped

2 T. green onions, chopped

1 T. nutritional yeast flakes

¼ t. Old Bay seasoning

salt to taste

Directions

In a medium bowl, mash the chickpeas with a fork until they have a coarse texture, or pulse in a food processor. Add remaining ingredients and mix well. Serve chilled.

Nutrition Facts

Serving Size	¼ c	Sodium	127mg
Calories	73	Carbs	11g
Fat	2g	Fiber	3g
Sat. Fat	0g	Sugar	2g
Cholesterol	0g	Protein	3.4g

Chicken Salad Sandwich

Prep	15-20 minutes
Bake	30 minutes
Makes	7 servings

INGREDIENTS

2 c. garbanzo beans, drained

¼ c. McKay's chicken seasoning

⅛ c. Bragg's Liquid Aminos or low-sodium soy sauce

2 ½ t. onion powder

½ t. salt

½ t. garlic powder

2 c. gluten flour, more if needed

Directions

In a blender, blend garbanzo beans with enough water from can to cover for 1-3 minutes. Add seasoning and blend until well mixed. Remove from blender or food processor and put into a large bowl. Slowly add gluten flour until it makes a firm dough. Form into patties and bake at 325° for 30 minutes, then flip patties over and bake an additional 20-30 minutes, or until golden.

To make it a salad, place patties into a food processor and pulse until the patties become large crumbles. Add onions, dill pickles, celery and vegan mayonnaise.

Nutrition Facts

Serving Size	½ c	Sodium	385mg
Calories	149	Carbs	19g
Fat	2g	Fiber	5g
Sat. Fat	<1g	Sugar	2.6g
Cholesterol	0g	Protein	14g

Manicotti

Prep   25 minutes

Cook   35 minutes

Makes   10 servings

Note: To make this recipe gluten-free, choose a gluten-free pasta. You can easily make a lasagna with this recipe by exchanging the manicotti pasta for lasagna noodles. Add well-drained, thawed spinach for some extra veggies.

INGREDIENTS

8 oz. manicotti, whole wheat if available

2¼ c. Tofu Ricotta cheese (p. 37)

¼ c. dairy-free sour cream of choice (p. 106)

3 T. parmesan cheese (pg. 107)

12-14 oz. tomato or spaghetti sauce of choice

Directions

Preheat oven to 350°. Prepare manicotti according to package. In a 9x13 baking dish, ladle ½ cup tomato or spaghetti sauce in bottom of dish. Cool off the manicotti by rinsing in cool water until you can handle the noodles. Spoon ricotta cheese filling into each shell, then place, layered, into the baking dish. Over the first layer, add ½ cup sauce and half the parmesan. Then put the remaining manicotti, sauce, and parmesan on top in layers.

Cover with parchment paper and aluminum foil, bake for 35 minutes. Remove the parchment paper and aluminum foil, bake for another 10-15 minutes, or until slightly golden.

Top with parmesan cheese, recipe on p. 107.

Nutrition Facts

Serving Size	1 shell	Sodium	286mg
Calories	170	Carbs	22g
Fat	6g	Fiber	3g
Sat. Fat	3g	Sugar	3g
Cholesterol	0g	Protein	10g

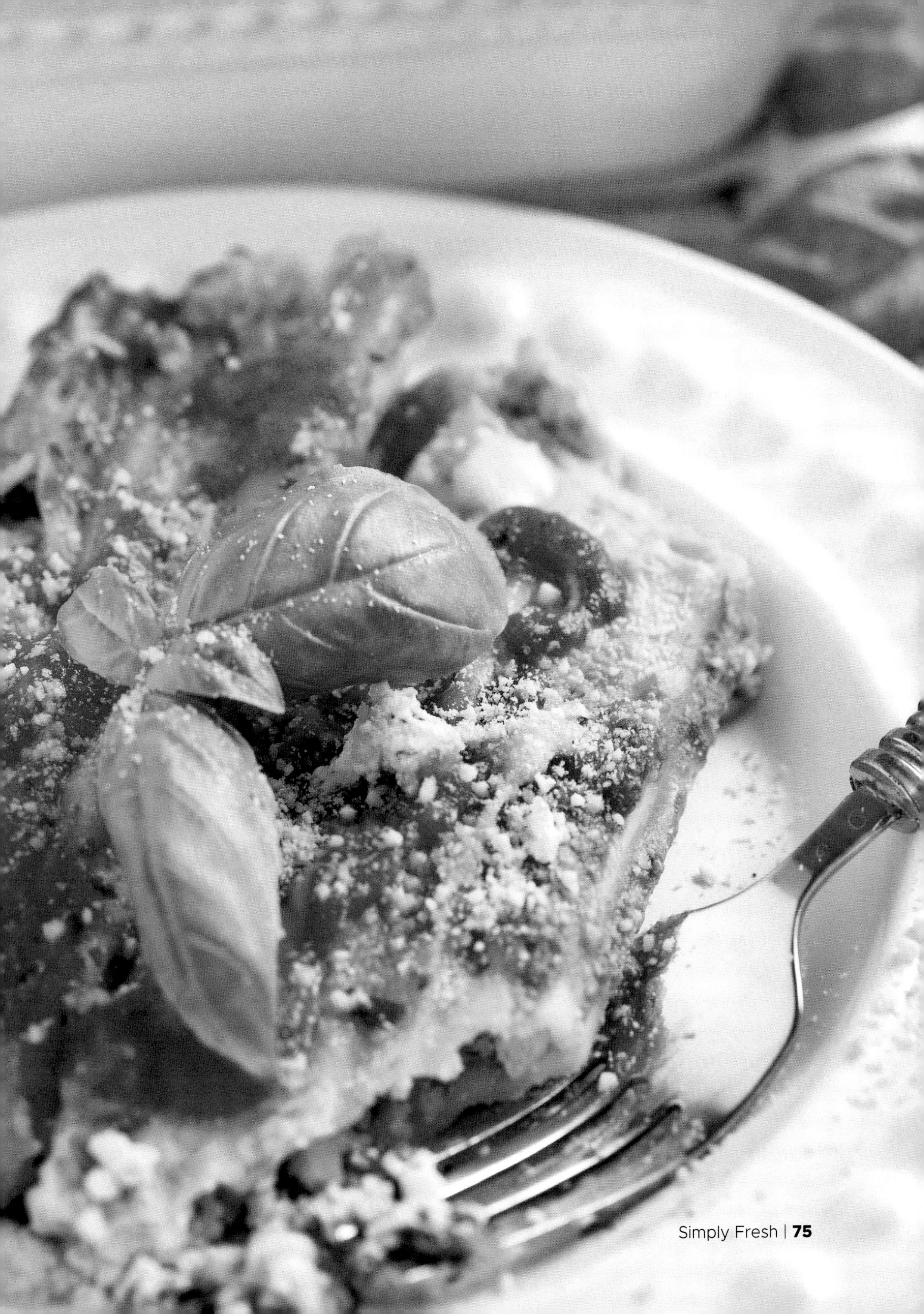

Mom's Pizza

Prep   30 minutes

Bake   15-20 minutes

Makes   12 servings

Note: To me, the more veggies the better, because they are what make this recipe great. To help keep the crust from getting soggy, try baking the crust for about 5-6 minutes, then add the sauce and veggies and continue to cook. Another technique is to add a small amount of olive oil between the dough crust and pesto sauce.

PIZZA DOUGH

2 ¼ t. active yeast (1 pkg.)

1 t. sugar

1 c. warm water (110˚)

2 ½ c. whole wheat pastry flour

2 T. olive oil

1 t. salt

2 T. corn meal

PIZZA TOPPINGS

½ red bell pepper

½ yellow bell pepper

½ orange bell pepper

1 c. packed fresh spinach

½ c. artichokes, chopped

1 tomato, diced

3 cloves garlic, minced

½ medium onion, diced

1 T. vegetable oil, or water

¼ - ½ c. pesto sauce (p. 104)

¼ t. salt, or to taste

For the dough

Preheat oven to 425˚. In a large bowl, mix yeast, sugar and warm water. Let stand for 5 minutes, or until bubbly. Add flour, salt and olive oil, then stir until well combined. Let rest for 10 minutes. Roll out the dough on a foured surface into a 12 inch crust. Place cornmeal on your surface and place dough on top, coating the bottom of the pizza dough. Place crust on perforated pizza pan or pizza stone. Top pizza with pesto sauce, then add sautéed toppings and tomatoes. Bake at 425˚ for 15-20 minutes or until crust is slightly golden.

For the toppings

In a large skillet, add the oil or water, onion and garlic and sauté for 3 minutes on a medium heat. Add the peppers and artichokes, sauté another 3 minutes. Add spinach and let it wilt down, which will take about 3-5 minutes. Set aside until dough is prepared.

Nutrition Facts

Serving Size	1 slice	Sodium	104mg
Calories	162	Carbs	22g
Fat	7g	Fiber	4g
Sat. Fat	1g	Sugar	0g
Cholesterol	0g	Protein	5g

Taco Meat

Prep   5 minutes
Cook   20 minutes
Makes   8 servings

INGREDIENTS

1 c. uncooked quinoa

1 t. oil or water for sautéeing

2 c. vegetable broth

½ t. salt, or to taste

1 t. taco seasoning

¼ c. onion, chopped

2 cloves garlic, diced

1 t. chili powder

½ t. ground cumin

¼ c. tomato sauce

Directions

Rinse uncooked quinoa and strain for two minutes. This helps to get rid of the quinoa flavor. Add quinoa to a large pot with oil or water, and cook on medium for 5 minutes until it is lightly browned. Add broth and bring to a boil. Turn heat down to low and let simmer for 20 minutes, or until the liquid is absorbed into the quinoa. Add the remaining ingredients and stir until well mixed. Cook for 5 more minutes or until the quinoa is crispy and resembles taco meat.

Nutrition Facts

Serving Size	¼ c	Sodium	207mg
Calories	95	Carbs	16g
Fat	2g	Fiber	2g
Sat. Fat	0g	Sugar	1g
Cholesterol	0g	Protein	7g

Italian Sausage

INGREDIENTS

2 ¼ c. vital wheat gluten
½ c. nutritional yeast flakes
¼ c. chickpea flour
3 T. McKay's chicken seasoning
2 T. onion powder
1 T. fennel seeds, optional
2 t. paprika
½ t. chili flakes (optional)
½ t. oregano
1 t. salt
2 ¼ c. cool water
6 cloves garlic, pressed or
   minced
2 T. olive oil
2 T. low-sodium soy sauce

Prep   20 minutes
Cook   30 minutes
Makes   10 servings

(NF) (SF) (D)

Directions

Mix all the dry ingredients in a large bowl. In a separate bowl, whisk the wet ingredients, including the garlic. Gently add the wet ingredients to the dry ingredients and stir until it is well combined. If the dough seems dry, slowly add more water until it is a big ball of dough. Place about ¼ - ½ cup of dough on a piece of parchment paper and roll it into log form. Wrap the parchment paper in aluminum foil and twist the ends. Continue until all dough is in sausage form. Steam the sausage rolls for 30 minutes. They should still be soft, but will harden during the cooling process.

These can be used as sausage rolls, or chop them up for sandwiches. There are many ways to use these sausages.

Nutrition Facts

Serving Size	1 link	Sodium	441mg
Calories	146	Carbs	13g
Fat	5g	Fiber	3g
Sat. Fat	<1g	Sugar	<1g
Cholesterol	0g	Protein	17g

BBQ Soy Curls

Prep   10 minutes

Cook   15 minutes

Makes   8 servings

Note: *Gluten-free if using a gluten-free barbeque sauce. For a great texture, be sure to sauté the soy curls until they are well browned, then add the BBQ sauce. Other sauces can be used with the soy curls. Try a sweet and sour for plant-based sweet-n-sour "chicken."*

INGREDIENTS

2 c. soy curls

1 ½ c. water

1 T. olive oil

½ - ¾ c. barbecue sauce

Directions

Soak the soy curls with water to rehydrate them. Drain the excess water.

On medium heat, add olive oil to the pan, then add soy curls. Allow them to cook for around 5-10 minutes, until they begin to become crispy.

Add the barbecue sauce and continute to cook for 5 minutes. Remove from heat and serve as desired.

Especially good as a sandwich.

Nutrition Facts

Serving Size	¼ c	Sodium	28mg
Calories	120	Carbs	8g
Fat	7g	Fiber	0.5g
Sat. Fat	<1g	Sugar	6g
Cholesterol	0g	Protein	9g

Macaroni & Cheese

Prep 7-10 minutes

Cook 20 minutes

Makes 8 servings

(GF) (SF) (D)

Note: To make this recipe gluten-free, use a gluten-free pasta. For an extra cheesy flavor, add extra nutritional yeast flakes.

INGREDIENTS

1 c. raw cashews

2 c. water

1 c. canned coconut milk

1 red bell pepper (or ½ a large)

¼ c. nutritional yeast flakes

1 t. onion powder

1 t. salt

¼ c. cornstarch

1 pkg. whole wheat macaroni shells

Directions

Cook pasta according to directions on box. Meanwhile, place remaining ingredients into a high-powered blender or food processor and blend until silky smooth. Once you strain your pasta, place it back into the pot and add the blended sauce.

Cook on medium heat until the sauce thickens and is the texture of macaroni and cheese, usually about 5-8 minutes. Stir continuously.

Serve.

Nutrition Facts

Serving Size	2 oz	Sodium	343mg
Calories	360	Carbs	55g
Fat	17g	Fiber	11g
Sat. Fat	8g	Sugar	4g
Cholesterol	0g	Protein	16g

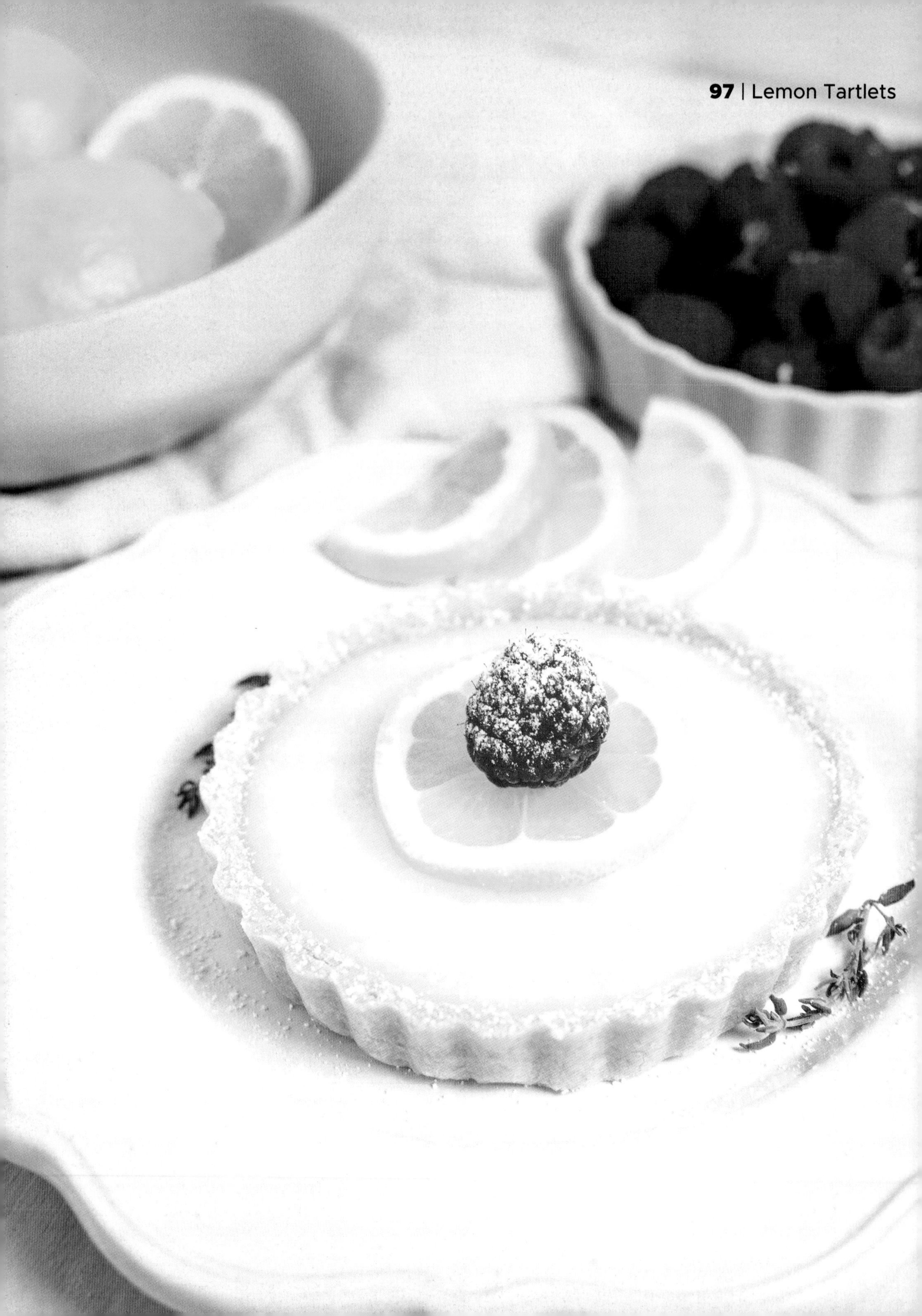

Dessert

Lemon Jewels

Prep 15-20 minutes

Makes 24 servings

(GF) (SF) (D)

Note: There are plenty of ways to mix up this recipe. Try using a different type of nut, nut butter, or other dried fruit. It's a great way to enjoy a protein-packed, guilt-free dessert.

INGREDIENTS

1 c. pitted dates, chopped

1 c. raw walnuts

1 c. sesame seeds

¼ c. lemon juice

2 t. freshly grated lemon zest

2 T. ground flaxseed

½ c. unsweetened dried coconut flakes

Directions

In a food processor place dates, walnuts, sesame seeds, flaxseed, lemon juice and zest. Pulse and blend until it is completely mixed. It will be slightly sticky. With moistened hands, roll tablespoons of the mixture into balls. Roll in coconut, then chill until ready to serve.

Nutrition Facts

Serving Size	1 ball	Sodium	5mg
Calories	89	Carbs	8g
Fat	6g	Fiber	2g
Sat. Fat	1g	Sugar	4.4g
Cholesterol	0g	Protein	2g

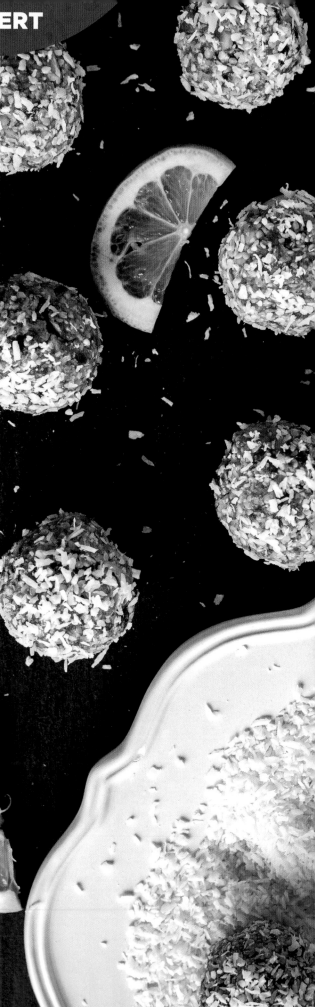

Orange Cranberry Scones

INGREDIENTS

2 c. all-purpose flour

7 t. sugar

1 T. grated orange peel

2 t. baking powder

½ t. salt

¼ t. baking soda

⅓ c. cold non-dairy butter

1 c. dried cranberries

¼ c. orange juice

1 T. ground flaxseed

¼ c. soy creamer

3 T. water

Glaze

½ c. powdered sugar

1 T. orange juice

Fruit Butter

⅓ c. non-dairy butter

2-3 T. jelly (orange would be best, but you can use any flavor)

Prep	15 minutes
Bake	12 minutes
Makes	12 servings

Directions

In a large bowl, combine flour, 7 teaspoons sugar, orange peel, baking powder, salt and baking soda. Cut in butter until the mixture resembles coarse crumbs, set aside. Combine the flaxseed and water. Set aside until you're ready to mix the dry and wet ingredients together. In a small bowl combine the cranberries, orange juice and cream. Add to flour mixture and stir until a soft dough forms.

On a floured surface, gently knead 6-8 times. Pat dough into an 8 inch circle. Cut into 10-12 wedges. Separate wedges and place on a lined baking sheet. Bake at 400° for 12 minutes. Combine ingredients for glaze. Brush scones with glaze. Put back in oven for approximately 3 more minutes, or until lightly browned. Remove to a wire rack to cool.

Combine ingredients for fruit butter. Serve fruit butter with warm scones.

Nutrition Facts

Serving Size	1 scone	Sodium	16mg
Calories	164	Carbs	27g
Fat	5g	Fiber	1g
Sat. Fat	<1g	Sugar	9g
Cholesterol	0g	Protein	2.6g

Key Lime Pie

Prep 15 minutes

Cook 10-12 minutes

Makes 10 servings

Note: Mix things up a bit and try making individual key lime tartlets. It's a fun way to enjoy this dessert. Top it off with twisted slice of lime and lime shavings to give it an elegant look.

INGREDIENTS

1 can white grape juice concentrate

12 oz. can coconut milk

⅔ c. cornstarch

1 brick silken tofu

⅓ c. maple syrup

⅛ c. lime juice

2 lime peels, grated

2 t. vanilla extract

2 pre-baked vegan pie crusts

DIRECTIONS

In a medium pot, place the white grape juice and cornstarch and mix together. Turn heat to medium, add coconut milk and bring to a boil, stirring constantly until it begins to boil and thicken.

In a blender, blend tofu, maple syrup, lime juice, vanilla, lemon extract and salt. Blend for 2-3 minutes or until it is smooth. Add thickened juice, blend slowly until well blended. Stir in the lime peel. Pour pie mixture evenly into pie shells and place in fridge until chilled.

Nutrition Facts

Serving Size	1 slice	Sodium	119mg
Calories	292	Carbs	29g
Fat	18g	Fiber	2g
Sat. Fat	9g	Sugar	<1g
Cholesterol	0g	Protein	6g

Pumpkin Cheesecake

Prep 8 minutes
Bake 45 minutes
Makes 10 Servings

(NF) (D)

PIE FILLING

12 oz. silken tofu
1 c. pumpkin
1 c. turbinado sugar
1 T. vanilla
3 T. flour
½ t. baking soda
1 ¼ t. pumpkin pie spice
8 oz. Tofutti cream cheese

CRUST

9 graham crackers
6 T. non-dairy butter, melted

Directions

Place graham crackers into a food processor and process until they are very fine. Add melted butter and process until it sticks together. Place in a pie pan and form crust with your hands.

In a blender, blend all pie filling ingredients for about 3-4 minutes. Pour into the pie crust. Bake at 350° for 45 minutes. Remove from heat, and refrigerate for 4 hours, or until chilled.

Nutrition Facts

Serving size	1 slice	Sodium	178mg
Calories	263	Carbs	32g
Fat	14g	Fiber	<1g
Sat. Fat	2g	Sugar	24g
Cholesterol	0g	Protein	3g

Blackberry Cobbler

Prep 15 minutes

Bake 30 minutes

Makes 12 servings

FILLING

36 oz. fresh or frozen blackberries

2 T. cornstarch

¼ c. maple syrup, agave nectar or honey

½ c. turbinado sugar

2 T. apricot jam

TOPPING

½ c. whole wheat flour

¼ t. salt

1 ½ c. oats

½ c. dairy-free butter, cold

½ t. cinnamon

Directions

Rinse fresh blackberries, add cornstarch, maple syrup, turbinado sugar and apricot jam, then mix together. Place in a 12" round pan and set aside while you prepare the crumble topping.

In a medium bowl, cut the butter into the flour with a pastry cutter or fork. Add salt, oats and cinnamon, then mix together until it resembles a coarse crumble.

Evenly pour the crumble topping over the blackberry mix. Bake at 350˚ for 30 minutes or until golden brown.

Nutrition Facts

Serving size	1 slice	Sodium	50mg
Calories	172	Carbs	36g
Fat	2g	Fiber	5g
Sat. Fat	0g	Sugar	17g
Cholesterol	0g	Protein	4g

Chocolate Pie

Prep 5 minutes

Cook 2+ hours

Makes 10 servings

(GF) (NF) (SF) (D)

Note: *This recipe is gluten-free if a gluten-free crust is used. Top this off with coconut whipped cream and dairy-free chocolate shavings to give it an elegant look.*

INGREDIENTS

1 lb. silken tofu

⅓ - ½ c. pure maple syrup

24 oz. vegan dark chocolate chips

1 pie crust (p. 98)

Directions

Drain water from tofu. Place tofu and maple syrup in a blender and blend about 3-4 minutes, or until completely smooth. Turn the burner on a low to medium heat and in a small sauce pan add the chocolate chips. Stir until the chips are melted. Add melted chocolate to the blender and blend for 2 minutes. Pour pie mixture into prepared pie crust. Put in the fridge for at least two hours, or until the pie is cooled down and set.

If you want, you can add soy or coconut whipped cream to the top of your pie to make it even more delicious.

Nutrition Facts

Serving size	1 slice	Sodium	99mg
Calories	423	Carbs	51g
Fat	23g	Fiber	4g
Sat. Fat	11g	Sugar	36g
Cholesterol	0g	Protein	0.7g

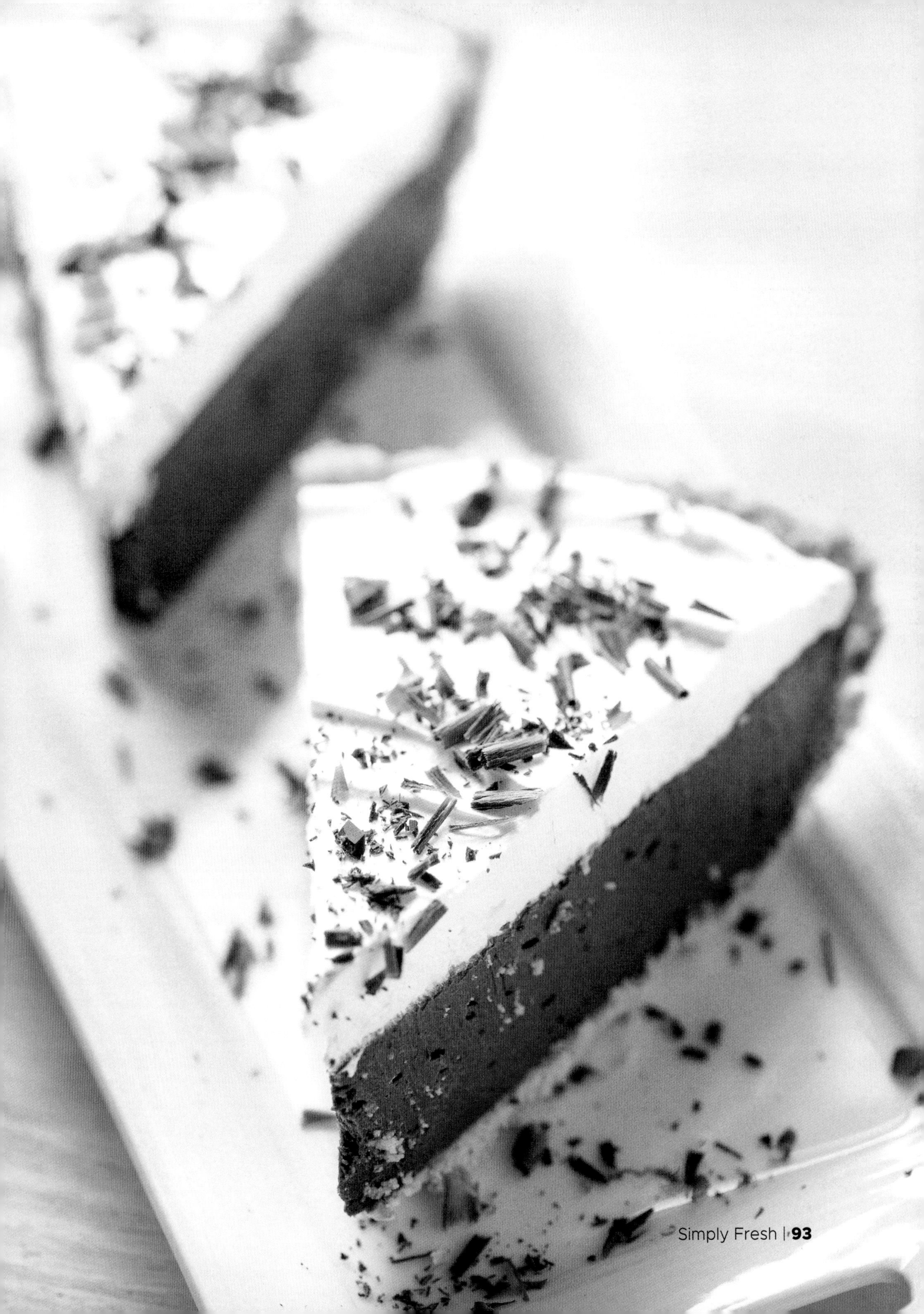

Coconut Tapioca

Prep   5 minutes

Cook   30-40 minutes

Makes   9 servings

(GF) (NF) (SF) (D)

Note: Tapioca comes from the root of the cassava plant. Typically it is used to thicken puddings, soups and fruit-pie fillings. This recipe is a great way to enjoy dessert without the guilt.

INGREDIENTS

32 oz. light coconut milk

⅓ c. maple syrup or honey

⅓ c. small pearl tapioca

1 t. coconut extract

1 t. vanilla extract

pinch of salt

Directions

Mix all ingredients well in a large saucepan. On a medium-high heat, bring to a boil, stirring frequently. Once it begins to boil, turn heat down to medium. Continue stirring until the tapioca pearls become clear. Place mixture in a serving bowl in the fridge until it is chilled.

During the chilling process, you can stir occasionally to help mix the tapioca evenly.

Nutrition Facts

Serving size	½ c	Sodium	16mg
Calories	69	Carbs	10g
Fat	3g	Fiber	0g
Sat. Fat	3g	Sugar	9g
Cholesterol	0g	Protein	<1g

Avocado Pudding

Prep 7-10 minutes

Makes 6 servings

(GF) (NF) (SF) (D)

INGREDIENTS

2 large, ripe avocados (about 1 lb.)

4 oz. chopped dairy-free chocolate (or chocolate chips)

3 T. unsweetened cocoa powder

¼ c. dairy-free milk

1 t. pure vanilla extract

5 pitted dates or 2 T. pure maple syrup

pinch of salt

Directions

Place chocolate in a microwave safe bowl, doing 15 second bursts and stirring between each burst. Once chocolate is almost all melted, set it aside to cool down for a few minutes.

Place avocados, pits and skins removed, into a food processor or blender. Add the melted chocolate, cocoa powder, dairy-free milk, vanilla extract, dates (or maple syrup), and salt. Blend until completely smooth. You will need to stop and scrape the sides. Taste test: if more sweetener is needed, add more maple syrup or dates as desired. Place into glasses or a bowl and serve chilled.

Serve with fresh strawberries, raspberries, and whipped coconut whipped cream. Add chocolate shavings to the top.

Nutrition Facts

Serving size	¼ c	Sodium	11mg
Calories	193	Carbs	23g
Fat	13g	Fiber	6g
Sat. Fat	4g	Sugar	14g
Cholesterol	0g	Protein	3g

Lemon Tartlets

Prep	15 minutes
Cook	25 minutes
Makes	12 servings

Note: To make this recipe soy-free, choose a non-dairy milk with no soy. To make it nut-free, use rice milk. Tartlets are great because they're just the right size for one person, but this recipe can easily be made into a lemon pie.

LEMON FILLING

13.5 oz. can coconut milk

½ c. turbinado sugar

pinch of salt

1 t. vanilla extract

1 ½ t. lemon extract

1 T. lemon juice

zest of two lemons

¼ c. dairy-free milk

¼ c. arrowroot or cornstarch

CRUST

1 ½ c. all-purpose flour

⅓ c. sugar

¼ t. salt

½ c. dairy-free butter

5-8 T. ice cold water

For the Crust

Preheat oven to 350˚. Place flour, sugar and salt into food processor. Once these ingredients are well mixed, add the butter. Pulse until mixture is crumbly. Add 5-8 tablespoons of ice cold water, until the dough forms a ball. Press the dough into a tart pan (or muffin pan). Bake for 20-25 minutes, or until edges turn golden. Let crust cool fully before filling.

For the Lemon filling

In a separate bowl, blend dairy-free milk and cornstarch. Make sure to mix well with a fork or whisk until there are no lumps. Set aside.

Place sugar, salt and coconut milk into a saucepan, and bring to a boil on medium-high heat, stirring occasionally. Once it begins to boil, reduce heat to medium and slowly add the cornstarch mixture. Whisk continuously. Continue to cook until it is the consistency of pudding, about 3-5 minutes.

Remove from heat and stir in remaining ingredients. Place filling into crust evenly. Place in fridge for 6-8 hours.

You may garnish with whichever fruit you like. I used raspberries.

Nutrition Facts

Serving size	1 tartlet	Cholesterol	0g	Sugar	14g
Calories	269	Sodium	56mg	Protein	2.5g
Fat	17g	Carbs	29g		
Sat. Fat	8g	Fiber	1g		

Pie Crust

Prep 15 minutes

Bake 10-15 minutes

Makes 10 servings

(NF) (SF) (D)

Note: Any pie crust will do, but this one has extra flavor and is full of wonderful nutrients. Plus, it contains fiber, so that's even less reason to feel guilty about dessert. If the crust seems a little too flakey and hard to roll out, try adding a little bit of water to make it more moldable.

INGREDIENTS

1 ½ cups whole wheat pastry flour

¾ cup rye flour

½ cup unbleached flour

¼ cup ground flaxseed

1 t. salt

⅔ cup canola oil

⅓ cup hot water

Directions

Mix together whole wheat pastry flour, rye flour, unbleached flour, flaxseed, and salt in a large bowl. Add oil and salt, then stir until well blended. Bake according to pie content instructions. If making a non-bake pie, bake pie crust at 350° for 10-15 minutes or until lightly golden.

Nutrition Facts

Serving size	1 slice	Sodium	248mg
Calories	205	Carbs	20g
Fat	13g	Fiber	3.4g
Sat. Fat	1g	Sugar	0g
Cholesterol	0g	Protein	4g

Fruit Roll-Ups

Prep 5 minutes

Cook 5-6 hours

Makes 8 servings

(GF) (NF) (SF) (D)

INGREDIENTS

2 c. ripe fruit (or frozen fruit)

2 t. lemon juice

2 T. agave nectar, or maple syrup

Directions

First, preheat oven to 180° or less. Place all the ingredients into a blender and blend until it is pureed and smooth. Pour onto lined baking sheet. You can use a sieve to strain out the seeds, or you can pour directly onto the pan. Place in oven for 5-6 hours, until the center is not tacky.

Once it is cooled off, peel it off and place onto parchment paper. Roll it up, then cut into 1" thick pieces.

Nutrition Facts

Serving size	1 roll	Sodium	0mg
Calories	23	Carbs	6g
Fat	0g	Fiber	1g
Sat. Fat	0g	Sugar	5g
Cholesterol	0g	Protein	0g

Coconut Whipped Cream

Prep 10 minutes

Makes 24 servings

(GF) (NF) (SF) (D)

INGREDIENTS

1 can coconut milk*, chilled overnight

½ t. vanilla

2-5 T. powdered sugar

Directions

In a kitchen aid or using a hand mixer, whip all ingredients together. Begin on a slow speed until the powdered sugar is mixed in, then turn up to help whip the coconut milk. Let it mix 3-5 minutes until it resembles the consistency of whipped cream.

* Do not use light coconut milk.

Nutrition Facts

Serving size	1 Tbsp	Sodium	0mg
Calories	14	Carbs	<1g
Fat	1g	Fiber	0g
Sat. Fat	1g	Sugar	<1g
Cholesterol	0g	Protein	0g

Banana Bread

Prep 10 minutes

Bake 50 minutes

Makes 12 servings

Note: If you do not have any dairy-free butter, you can try using ¼ cup vegetable oil or 1/3 cup unsweetened applesauce. It may change the taste and texture a little bit, but these are good substitutes to keep in mind.

INGREDIENTS

3 bananas, spotted and overripe

⅓ c. melted dairy-free butter

¾ c. sugar

1 t. vanilla

1 t. baking soda

pinch of salt

1 ½ c. all-purpose flour

3 T. water mixed with 1 T. ground flaxseed

Directions

Preheat oven to 350°, and butter a bread pan. In a mixing bowl, mash the three bananas with a fork until smooth. Add the melted dairy-free butter into the mashed bananas.

Mix in the baking soda, salt, sugar, vanilla and flaxseed combination. Finally, mix in the flour, just until it is completely blended.

Pour the batter into your prepared bread pan. Bake at 350° for one hour. At 50 minutes, check the loaf to see if it is finished, by poking a toothpick or knife in the middle of the loaf. If it comes out clean the bread is finished, if it has batter, cook the remaining ten minutes.

Remove the banana bread from the oven and place on a cooling rack. Remove the bread from the pan, slice and serve.

Nutrition Facts

Serving size	1 slice	Sodium	118mg
Calories	177	Carbs	31g
Fat	5g	Fiber	1.4g
Sat. Fat	<1g	Sugar	16g
Cholesterol	0g	Protein	2g

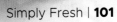

Basics

Ketchup

Mayonnaise

Prep 5 minutes
Makes 24 servings

Prep 5 minutes
Makes 10 servings

INGREDIENTS

1 c. tomato puree

¼ c. maple syrup

½ t. garlic

2 T. lemon juice

1 t. salt

½ t. onion powder

½ t. paprika

¼ t. oregano

⅛ t. cayenne pepper (optional)

INGREDIENTS

½ c. raw cashews

½ c. water

½ t. garlic powder

½ t. salt

1 t. onion powder

3 T. lemon juice

Directions

Place all ingredients in a blender and blend for 3-5 minutes, or until smooth.

Directions

In a bowl, combine all ingredients, stir until well combined. Serve chilled.

Nutrition Facts

Serving size	1 Tbsp	Sodium	100mg
Calories	13	Carbs	3g
Fat	<1g	Fiber	0g
Sat. Fat	0g	Sugar	3g
Cholesterol	0g	Protein	0g

Nutrition Facts

Serving size	2 Tbsp	Sodium	118mg
Calories	32	Carbs	2g
Fat	2g	Fiber	<1g
Sat. Fat	0g	Sugar	<1g
Cholesterol	0g	Protein	1g

Pesto Sauce

Prep   8-10 minutes

Makes   16 servings

(GF) (SF) (D)

Note: This sauce has a bold flavor, which is why you do not need a large amount for your pasta, sandwich or pizza. A little bit goes a long way.

INGREDIENTS

2 c. basil, packed

¼ c. pine nuts (or walnuts)

2 T. nutritional yeast flakes

1 T. lemon juice

2 cloves of garlic

¼ c. olive oil

salt to taste

Directions

Place basil, pine nuts, yeast flakes, lemon juice, garlic and salt into a food processor. Blend on a medium speed while slowly adding the olive oil. If needed, more olive oil may be added until it is the perfect consistency. Eat with pasta, as a pizza sauce, or my favorite, Israeli couscous.

Nutrition Facts

Serving size	1 Tbsp	Sodium	10mg
Calories	48	Carbs	<1g
Fat	5g	Fiber	0g
Sat. Fat	<1g	Sugar	0g
Cholesterol	0g	Protein	<1g

Cilantro Dressing

Prep 5 minutes

Makes 16 servings

(GF) (NF) (SF) (D)

INGREDIENTS

1 c. loosely packed cilantro, stems removed and roughly chopped

½ avocado (or ½ c. dairy-free yogurt)

¼ c. lemon juice

1-2 garlic cloves

¼ c. olive oil

¼ t. salt

Directions

Place all ingredients in a blender, and blend for about 2-3 minutes until smooth. Taste and adjust seasonings if necessary.

Nutrition Facts

Serving size	1 Tbsp	Sodium	37mg
Calories	38	Carbs	<1g
Fat	4g	Fiber	0g
Sat. Fat	<1g	Sugar	0g
Cholesterol	0g	Protein	0g

Ranch Dressing

Prep 10 minutes

Makes 16 servings

(GF) (NF) (SF) (D)

Note: To make this dressing soy-free, use a mayonnaise with no soy.

INGREDIENTS

1 c. mayonnaise of choice (p. 103)

1 T. dried parsley

½ t. salt

1 t. onion powder

½ t. garlic powder

1 T. fresh dill

2 T. lemon juice

Directions

Combine all ingredients in a bowl. Mix well and serve chilled.

Nutrition Facts

Serving size	1 Tbsp	Sodium	189mg
Calories	50	Carbs	1g
Fat	5g	Fiber	0g
Sat. Fat	0g	Sugar	0g
Cholesterol	0g	Protein	1g

BBQ Sauce

(GF) (NF) (SF) (D)

Prep 7 minutes

Cook 20 minutes

Makes 24 servings

INGREDIENTS

1 ½ cups tomato sauce

¼ cup date paste (blended dates)

1 T onion powder

1 t smoked paprika

1 t liquid smoke

1 t chili powder

1 t dried oregano

Directions

Place all ingredients into blender and blend for 3-4 minutes or until smooth. Add to small sauce pan and bring to boil. Reduce heat to low and allow to simmer for 15 minutes. Serve chilled.

Nutrition Facts

Serving Size	1 Tbsp	Sodium	64mg
Calories	12 g	Carbs	2 g
Fat	<1 g	Fiber	.5 g
Sat. Fat	0 g	Sugar	2 g
Cholesterol	0 g	Protein	0 g

Sour Cream

(GF) (NF) (D)

Prep 5 minutes

Serves 40 servings

INGREDIENTS

1 pkg. soft tofu, drained

¼ c. olive oil

1 clove garlic

1 t. salt

1 t. onion powder

1 ½ T. lemon juice

Directions

Place all ingredients in a blender, and blend for about 3-4 minutes, or until smooth. Store in refrigerator to chill.

Alternative recipe on p. 117

Nutrition Facts

Serving size	1 Tbsp	Sodium	59mg
Calories	18	Carbs	0g
Fat	2g	Fiber	0g
Sat. Fat	0g	Sugar	0g
Cholesterol	0g	Protein	<1g

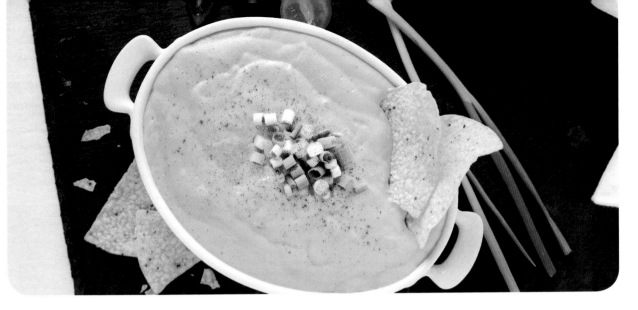

Nacho Cheese

Prep   5 minutes

Cook   10-12 minutes

Makes   12 servings

(GF) (SF) (D)

INGREDIENTS

1 c. raw cashews

2 c. water

1 red bell pepper, de-seeded

3 T. nutritional yeast flakes

2 t. onion powder

1 ½ t. salt

½ t. garlic powder

Directions

Place cashews and water into blender and blend until smooth, about 3-4 minutes. Add remaining ingredients and blend for another 3-4 minutes, until smooth. Place in medium pot and heat on medium, stirring constantly. Bring to a boil and continue stirring for one more minute, then remove from heat. It should be the consistency of nacho cheese. Serve hot.

If you are using this recipe for a lasagna you will not need to heat it in a pot before. It will stay good in the refrigerator for 3-5 days.

Parmesan

Prep   8-10 minutes

Makes   13 servings

(GF) (SF) (D)

INGREDIENTS

¾ c. raw cashews

3 T. nutritional yeast flakes

½ t. salt

¼ t. garlic powder

Directions

In a food processor, combine all the ingredients and pulse until it becomes a fine meal. It should resemble the consistency of parmesan cheese. It will last for several weeks if stored in the refrigerator.

Nutrition Facts | Parmesan

Serving size	1 Tbsp	Sodium	92mg
Calories	53	Carbs	3g
Fat	4g	Fiber	1g
Sat. Fat	<1g	Sugar	0g
Cholesterol	0g	Protein	2.4g

Nutrition Facts | Nacho Cheese

Serving size	¼ c	Sodium	197mg
Calories	72	Carbs	5g
Fat	5g	Fiber	1g
Sat. Fat	<1g	Sugar	<1g
Cholesterol	0g	Protein	2.6g

Drinks & Juicing

Chocolate Peanut Butter Shake

Prep 5 minutes

Makes 2 servings

(GF) (SF) (D)

Note: To make this treat extra packed with protien, try replacing the cocoa powder with a chocolate-flavored plant-based protien powder. To make this recipe soy-free, choose a milk that does not contain soy.

INGREDIENTS

1 cup non-dairy milk

2 frozen bananas

3 dates

1 T. cocoa powder

1 T. peanut butter

Directions

Place all ingredients in a blender, and blend for about 3-5 minutes, or until smooth and creamy.

Nutrition Facts

Serving Size	½ recipe	Sodium	88mg
Calories	244	Carbs	44g
Fat	7g	Fiber	5.5g
Sat. Fat	1.5g	Sugar	26.5g
Cholesterol	0g	Protein	7g

Pineapple Mint Juice

Prep 8 minutes

Makes 2 servings

(GF) (NF) (SF)

Note: *You can either enjoy as a smoothie right away or wait an hour as it settles to enjoy as fresh juice.*

INGREDIENTS

½ fresh pineapple

handful of fresh mint leaves

1 lemon, juiced

1 cup of ice

1 T agave, optional

Directions

Place all ingredients in blender and blend for 3-5 minutes until smooth.

Nutrition Facts

Serving Size	½ recipe	Sodium	5mg
Calories	159	Carbs	42g
Fat	<1g	Fiber	5g
Sat. Fat	0g	Sugar	30g
Cholesterol	0g	Protein	2g

Ginger Ale

Prep 10 minutes

Makes 36 ounces

(GF) (NF) (SF) (D)

INGREDIENTS

3-4 inches of fresh ginger, skin removed

½ cup fresh lemon juice

32oz sparkling water

Pure maple syrup or other nautral sweetner, to taste

Directions

Peel the ginger skin and place ginger in a blender along with the lemon juice. Blend until smooth, about 2-3 minutes. Add ½ cup of sparkling water and continue to blend for another minute or two. Strain juice with a fine strainer into a pitcher. Add the rest of the sparkling water. To sweeten, add pure maple syrup or other sweetner.

Nutrition Facts

Serving Size	8oz	Sodium	1mg
Calories	32	Carbs	8g
Fat	0g	Fiber	0g
Sat. Fat	0g	Sugar	8g
Cholesterol	0g	Protein	0g

Juicing and it's Benefits

Juice fasting is a way to give your body a break, while filling it with much-needed nutrients. Juicing does not have to leave a bad taste in your mouth, literally. It's important to enjoy the foods/juices you put into your body, as well as making sure they are beneficial.

Juicing can give the body the nutrients that it needs in a quick manner. The vitamins, minerals, enzymes, phytonutrients, carbohydrates, chlorophyll, etc. can help to increase health and healing.

The body is amazing and is able to heal itself, especially when given the proper nutrients. I have personally experienced the healing power of juicing. A couple years ago I was starting to have symptoms of appendicitis (inflammation of the appendix). I figured it would be wise to get food that fights against inflammation. After drinking a large glass of fresh juice, I went to the emergency room. From the CT scan it was clear that I had appendicitis, and the doctor had recommended surgery as soon as possible.

While waiting for a surgical unit to open, I decided to rest. After taking a two-hour nap, I woke up with no pain. I let the doctor know that I was no longer experiencing pain or symptoms of appendicitis. I also let him know about the anti-inflammatory foods that I had juiced. Though he still highly recommended the surgery, I declined and went home to continue juicing. I continued juicing for an additional three days, consuming only juice to see if it would continue to heal my appendicitis. It was then suggested that I get a second opinion from another surgeon. Two days later, the second surgeon told me that I was no longer showing signs or symptoms of appendicitis. I'm happy to say that my appendix is still with me, and I have not had any troubles with it since.

The power of food is real, which is why it's important to feed our bodies as best we can. Here you'll find some great options for anyone wanting to do a three-day detox, or to get extra nutrients any time you need the boost.

GET STARTED: Your body can get a lot of benefit from three days of juicing. Take your pick and plan to juice 3-5 times a day. Need more? Make another juice.

Tropical Breakfast

Benefits: This contains beta-cerotine, vitamin C, calcium, magnesium, folic acid, manganese, phosphorus, potassium, and sulphur. It helps aid in digestion, helps the skin, and gives energy.

INGREDIENTS

3 apples

½ pineapple

1 lime, peeled

1 passion fruit

Breakfast That Bites

Benefits: Includes beta-carotene, vitamin C, folic acid, calcium, phosphorus, potassium, magnesium, and sulphur. It's great for energy, detox, building the immune system, aids in digestion, and is beneficial to the skin.

INGREDIENTS

3 apples

2 carrots

½ inch ginger root

½ lime, peeled

Grateful Start

Benefits: A great source for beta-carotene, biotin, vitamin C, folic acid, phosphorus, potassium, magnesium, manganese, sodium, and sulphur. It's great for energy, building the immune system, and is beneficial to the skin.

INGREDIENTS

3 apples

½ pineapple

1 lime, peeled

1 passion fruit

Red Carrots

Benefits: *This is great for detoxification and cleansing. Contains beta-carotene, folic acid, iron, calcium, magnesium, manganese, phosphorus, potassium, sodium, sulphur, and vitamins B3, B6, and C.*

INGREDIENTS

3 carrots

1 apple

1 orange, peeled

½ beet

1 celery stick

2 large kale leaves

Cold Kicker

Benefits: *Garlic is a great way to boost the immune system and help fight off a cold. Contains beta-carotene, folic acid, vitamin C, calcium, potassium, magnesium, phosphorus, and sulphur.*

INGREDIENTS

2 grapefruits, peeled

1 lemon, peeled

1 inch fresh ginger

1 garlic clove

Peachy Fresh

Benefits: *This is a great juice for energy and is helpful for the skin. Contains beta-carotene, folic acid, calcium, magnesium, phosphorus, potassium, sodium, sulphur, and vitamins B3 and C.*

INGREDIENTS

3 peaches

1 apple

1 lemon, peeled

1 small bunch fresh mint

JUICING TIP: Juicing is a great way to give your body a power-punch of nutrients. Just drinking one juice can support immunity, improve your energy, and refresh your system.

Fresh Veggies

Benefits: This helps to detoxify and is good for the skin. Contains beta-carotene, biotin, folic acid, calcium, iron, magnesium, phosphorus, potassium, sodium, sulphur, and vitamins B3 and C.

INGREDIENTS

1 cucumber

3 tomatoes

1 small bunch fresh parsley

1 lemon, peeled

Stomach Soother

Benefits: This is great for the digestive tract. Contains beta-carotene, folic acid, calcium, magnesium, managnese, phosphorus, potassium, sodium, sulphur, and vitamin C.

INGREDIENTS

2 pears

3 carrots

½ pineapple

½ inch fresh ginger

Anti-Inflammatory

Benefits: Helps fight against inflammation. Contains beta-carotine, calcium, potassium, sodium, copper, phosphorus, magnesium, folate, and vitamin C.

INGREDIENTS

2 beets

1 cucumber

1 inch fresh ginger

2 apples

2 lemons

Plant-based Eating

PLANT-BASED PROTIEN

These days we are programed to think that protein is only found in meat and animal products. Many people ask the question, "Where do you get your protein if you are a plant-based vegetarian?" The answer is: In everything we eat. All plants have protein in them.

The fact is, the average American is consuming *too much* protein in their diets. Many of the fad diets tend to include high amounts of protein, usually from meat. There is actually a five-fold increase risk of diabetes mortality in those found to be eating the highest protein intake, according to a 2014 study. However, the mortality was associated only with animal protein. The risk of disease disappeared if the protein came from plant foods.

Eating excess protein can lead to a deterioration in kidney function. This is especially important for people with diabetes, since there is already a higher risk of kidney damage. Animal protein also contains cholesterol and raises the cholesterol levels, whereas plant proteins do not contain cholesterol and actually help to lower cholesterol levels.

Proteins are made up of amino acids. These are essential nutrients for the body to synthesize its own protein. They help to form and maintain the tissues, defend against infection, form blood hemoglobin, produces enzymes, and gives energy. There are 9 essential amino acids to make up a complete protein, something that is necessary for good health.

Daily Value (Recommended Dietary Allowance) of proteins for the average adult is 50 grams of protein.

Based on caloric intake: 10% comes from proteins. The maximum is 15%. Based on a 2,000 calorie diet, the amount would be 50 grams, with a maximum of 75 grams.

Consequences of excess protein:

Too much protein can cause kidney issues, liver problems, damage to the lining of the arteries (leads to plaque build-up), and other health issues. Other disease can occur when excess protein is consumed: rheumatic disease, gout, and acidification of the blood.

Consequences of protein deficiency:

When not consuming enough protein some symptoms can be weakness, lethargy, depressed immune system, edema, and liver failure.

The great thing about plant-based protein is that they do not contain cholesterol, unhealthy fats, and are low in sodium. Below is a chart of some of the plant foods that contain protein and how much they contain per serving. There are plenty of ways to make sure you are getting enough protein during the day.

Lentils 18 g per cup

Edamame 18 g per cup

Beans 12-15 g per cup

Tofu 8-15 g per 3 oz.

Quinoa 11 g per cup

Nut butter 7 g per 2 tablespoons

Almonds 6 g per ¼ cup

Chia seed 6 g per 2 tablespoons

Steel-cut oats 5 g per ¼ cup

Potato 4 g per 1 medium white potato

Wheat bread 4 g per slice

Spinach 3 g per ½ cup serving

Corn 2.5 g per ½ cup

Avocado 2 g per ½ avocado

Broccoli 2 g per ½ cup (cooked)

Flaxseed, ground, 1.3 g per tablespoon

STEAMING VEGETABLES

Steaming is a quick and simple way to cook vegetables. It adds color, texture, retains flavor, and has better nutritional content that some other methods of cooking vegetables. When cooking vegetables, steaming on the stovetop using a steamer basket is the best option. This helps to keep the water-soluble vitamins (B and C) in the vegetables. Adding water to a pot and placing the vegetables directly into the water causes the majority of the water-soluble vitamins to be excreted to the water. Using a steamer basket, which holds the vegetables out of the water, allows the steam to cook them, which helps to hold in the water-soluble vitamins.

For more information and specific steaming instructions for various vegetables, visit the website at: www.kyleeskitchen.com/simplyfresh/steaming.

SUBSTITUTING FOR PLANT FOODS

Butter

Coconut oil

⅓ cup vegetable oil = 1 stick butter

Non-hydrogenated butter, such as Earth Balance or Smart Balance

Cheese

Cashew Nacho Cheese sauce (p. 107)

Tofu Ricotta Cheese (p. 37)

Nutritional yeast flakes

Non-dairy store-bought cheeses: Daiya, Follow Your Heart, Chao, Tofutti, Miyoko's, Go-Veggie, etc.

Condensed Milk

1 can coconut milk + ¼ c. sugar

Eggs

1 tablespoon ground flaxseed + 3 tablespoons water = 1 egg (combine, set for 3-5 minutes)

Ener G Egg Replacer (can be found in a health food store, or some grocery stores)

½ ripe banana, smashed =1 egg

¼ cup applesauce

Tofu, best for egg dishes such as quiche, frittata, or egg salad.

1 teaspoon baking soda + 1 tablespoon white vinegar = 1 egg (Use only in baking)

Heavy Cream

Coconut cream: Let a full can of full-fat coconut milk settle for about 30 minutes. The coconut cream will be at the top of the can, making it easy to be skimmed off. Use only the coconut cream.

Silken tofu, blended (use a 1:1 ratio)

½ cup non-dairy milk + ½ cup canola oil = 1 cup heavy cream

Mayonnaise

Dairy-free mayonnaise recipe (p. 103)

Vegenaise (found at most grocery stores)

Nayonaise (found at health food stores)

Just Mayo (found at most grocery stores)

Meat

Tofu, seitan, mushrooms, tempeh, beans, soy curls, store bought vegan meat substitutes.

Meat broth

Vegetable broth

1 quart water + 1 ½ teaspoons McKay's Seasoning = 1 quart meat broth

Vegetable bouillon cubes (prepare as directed)

Milk

Soy milk, almond milk, cashew milk, rice milk, coconut milk, hemp milk, oat milk

Refined Sugar

Dried fruit, applesauce, turbinado sugar (made from the initial pressing of the sugar cane)

Sour Cream

Tofutti Sour Cream

Blend 1 cup cashews, 2 teaspoons apple cider vinegar, 1 teaspoon lemon juice, pinch of salt

FOOD DIARY

Saturday

Vegetables
( ) ( ) ( ) ( ) ( ) ( )
Fruits
( ) ( ) ( ) ( ) ( ) ( )
Whole Grains
( ) ( ) ( ) ( ) ( ) ( )
Protiens ( ) ( ) ( )
N.D. Milk ( ) ( )

Friday

Vegetables
( ) ( ) ( ) ( ) ( ) ( )
Fruits
( ) ( ) ( ) ( ) ( ) ( )
Whole Grains
( ) ( ) ( ) ( ) ( )
Protiens ( ) ( ) ( )
N.D. Milk ( ) ( )

Thursday

Vegetables
( ) ( ) ( ) ( ) ( ) ( )
Fruits
( ) ( ) ( ) ( ) ( )
Whole Grains
( ) ( ) ( ) ( ) ( )
Protiens ( ) ( ) ( )
N.D. Milk ( ) ( )

Wednesday

Vegetables
( ) ( ) ( ) ( ) ( )
Fruits
( ) ( ) ( ) ( ) ( )
Whole Grains
( ) ( ) ( ) ( )
Protiens ( ) ( ) ( )
N.D. Milk ( ) ( )

Tuesday

Vegetables
( ) ( ) ( ) ( ) ( )
Fruits
( ) ( ) ( ) ( ) ( )
Whole Grains
( ) ( ) ( ) ( )
Protiens ( ) ( ) ( )
N.D. Milk ( ) ( )

Monday

Vegetables
( ) ( ) ( ) ( ) ( )
Fruits
( ) ( ) ( ) ( ) ( )
Whole Grains
( ) ( ) ( ) ( )
Protiens ( ) ( ) ( )
N.D. Milk ( ) ( )

Sunday

Vegetables
( ) ( ) ( ) ( )
Fruits
( ) ( ) ( ) ( )
Whole Grains
( ) ( ) ( ) ( )
Protiens ( ) ( ) ( )
N.D. Milk ( ) ( )

Totals

Breakfast

Lunch & Snacks

Dinner

For more ideas on menu planning, visit:
www.typofire.com/fresh/menuplan

	Sunday	Monday	Tuesday	Wednesday	Thursday	Friday	Saturday
Breakfast	Scambled tofu, 2 corn tortillas, 2 T. salsa, 1 apple	1 cup Crockpot Oats, 2T. Dried fruit, 1/2 c. Fresh fruit, 1 oz. Nuts	2 Pancakes, 2 T. Pure maple syrup, 1/2 c. Applesauce, 1/2 Banana	1 c. Chia Pudding, 1/2 c. Fresh Fruit, 1 slice, Wheat Toast, 1 oz. Nuts	1 cup Pumpkin pie oatmeal, 1 medium Orange, 1 oz. Nuts	2 Biscuits, 1/2 cup Gravy, 2 Sausage Patties, 1 piece small Fruit	1 cup Overnight Muesli, 1 oz. Nuts
Lunch	1 cup Macaroni & cheese, Black beans, Raw veggies	3 Tofu lettuce wraps, 1/2 cup rice	2 Pieces, manicotti, 2 c. Green salad, 1 T. Dressing	1 c. Pumpin Pie Oatmeal, 1 medium Orange, 1 oz. Nuts	1 Oat burger, 1 Whole Wheat bun, 1 T. Ketchup, 1/2 Brazilian potato salad	1 1/2 c. Rosemary Potato Soup, 1 c. Corn & Edamame Salad	1/2 cup Black beans, 1/2 cup Brown rice, 2 cups Super Kale Salad
Dinner	2 cups Vegetable soup, 2 cups seasoned popcorn	1 cup Cucumber dill salad, 1 Eggless salad sandwich	1 c. Fruit salad, 1 Chicken salad sandwich	1 1/2 c. Navy Bean Soup, 1 piece Corn Bread	1/2 cup Taco Meat, 2 small Tortillas, 2 T. Salsa, 3 slices Avocado	2 cups Anti-Inflammatory juice, 2 cups Southwestern salad	1 1/2 cup Cauliflower soup, 1 piece Chocolate pie

INDEX

General Index

Health Benefits

Reduces Inflammation

Good for Digestion

Heart Healthy

INDEX

INDEX

INDEX

A

Agave Nectar is about 1.5 times sweeter than regular sugar and comes from the agave plant, which is also used to make tequila. It is a plant that is found mostly in the southwestern U.S. and the northern territory of South America. It is mostly fructose and is highly processed before the final product is finished.

Aluminum-free Baking Powder Baking powder usually contains aluminum, however this is an aluminum-free product. Aluminum has been proven to cause health problems. Featherweight or Rumford brands work well.

Arrowroot is used in place of cornstarch and acts as a thickening agent. It is a fine powder that comes from the rootstock of a tropical tuber. It is a corn-free alternative to cornstarch, and can be used interchangeably.

B

Beef-Style Seasoning, McKay's An all-purpose seasoning that gives a beef-like flavor to vegetarian cooking. There are other vegan beef style seasonings out there, but I prefer McKay's.

Bragg's Liquid Aminos is a non-fermented soy sauce that tends to be lower in sodium than other soy sauces. It can be used in place of soy sauce.

C

Chia Seed has a unique gelling action. They can be used as an egg replacer in baking or thickening puddings. There are many health benefits to chia seeds, and they are a great source of omega-3 fatty acids.

Chicken Style Seasoning, McKay's is an all-purpose seasoning that gives a chicken-like flavor to vegetarian cooking. There are other vegan chicken style seasonings out there, but I prefer McKay's.

Coconut Milk Canned coconut milk adds a creamy and rich quality to recipes to help to mimic dairy cream. It's important to use full-fat coconut milk when substituting for dairy cream in recipes. Look on the nutrition labels of the cans of coconut milk and make sure they have at least 16% fat.

D

Dairy-Free Butter There are a few different types of non-dairy butters on the market. Earth Balance is a great non-dairy substitute for butter or margarine. It is a non-hydrogenated product that has great flavor. Make sure to read the labels of non-dairy butters because some can contain whey (a milk product) or fish oil (promoting omega-3).

Dairy-Free Mayonnaise There are a few to chose from these days. They contain no cholesterol. Vegenaise or Just Mayo are good brands.

Dairy-Free Milk Soy Milk is made from soybeans and water, this contains almost as much protein as cow's milk. It is free of cholesterol and saturated fat. Almond Milk is made from almonds and water. It is low in calories, contains no cholesterol or saturated fat. It is not a good source of protein, however. Cashew Milk is made from cashews and water. This is a creamy substitute for milk. It is free of cholesterol and saturated fat. Rice Milk is a great alternative for those allergic to nuts or soy. It is a thinner type of milk and is enriched with vitamins. It is free of cholesterol and saturated fat.

Dairy-Free Yogurt There are soy, coconut, and almond yogurts that can be purchased at most grocery stores. They come in a variety of flavors and can be used in place of other dairy yogurts.

E

Egg Replacer, Ener-G It is made from starch and can be used in place of eggs in baking. It can be found in health food stores.

F

Flax Seed This has a gelling property and is usually used in place of eggs in baking. It is a great source of omega-3 fatty acids. Be sure to grind the whole flaxseed or use flaxseed meal, because the digestive system is not able to breakdown the whole seeds. Typically I will grind my own whole flaxseeds in a coffee grinder, and make enough to use for a week or so. It is best kept in the refrigerator in an air-tight sealed container.

G

Gluten Flour Best known as vital wheat gluten. It comes from the wheat kernel which contains almost all the protein.

L

Liquid Smoke
It is a water-soluble liquid used for flavoring and gives off a smoke or barbecue taste.

N

Nutritional Yeast Flakes have a cheesy flavor to them and are great to use in recipes that need a cheese flavor. They contain B-vitamins, including B12, which is an important vitamin for those who do not eat dairy or meat.

O

Old Bay Seasoning is a blend of herbs and spices that is used to mimic a seafood flavoring.

P

Pure Maple Syrup is made from the maple tree sap. There are grade A or B, light, or medium types, and they can all be used in these recipes. Make sure to use the 100% pure maple syrup. Other maples syrups are loaded with added sugar or high fructose corn syrup. Pure maple syrup is a bit more expensive, but it is worth the price.

Q

Quinoa is a tiny grain that contains all essential amino acids, and is considered a complete protein. It cooks quickly (15-20 minutes) and can be used in place of rice, or mixed with brown rice. It is considered to be a superfood and contains great nutrition.

R

Raw Cashews are cashews that have not been roasted or salted. These give less flavor and a more creamy texture to recipes. These are a a great source of antioxidants and protein.

S

Soy Curls are made from the whole soybean. These are a great meat substitute. They come dried, so they require re-hydration and seasonings.

Soy Creamer is a dairy-free creamer made by Silk. It is great to use in place of half-and-half or other recipes that require dairy creamer.

Soy Cream Cheese
There are a few dairy-free brands available. It has a creamy rich texture and can be used for cream cheese.

Soy Sour Cream can be used in place of any sour cream recipe. My favorite brand is the Tofutti "Better than Sour Cream." It is a non-hydrogenated oil product.

Sucanat is dried sugar cane juice that retains its molasses content, similar to brown sugar. It is a bit grainier than brown sugar. It is best used in place of sugar.

T

Tofu
It is made from soybeans. Mostly it is flavorless so it's important to season well.
For those who do not eat meat this is a great alternative since it is high in protein and iron, and is very low in calories and fat. There are different kinds of tofu ranging from soft to extra firm. The extra firm tofu is good for crumbling, baking, and stir-frying. Silken tofu is best for baking or using in smoothies, since the texture is very creamy.

Turbinado Sugar
Also known as Sugar in the Raw, is a golden-colored raw cane sugar. No chemicals, bone char or animal by-products are used in this product.

V

Vegenaise is a vegan alternative to mayonnaise. It contains no cholesterol and is plant based. Vegenaise from Follow Your Heart is my favorite brand to use. It can be found in health food stores as well as some grocery stores.

W

Whole Wheat Flour is a perfect flour for breads since it has a high gluten content. It is made from the whole wheat berry and contains all the vitamins and nutrients that are found in wheat, unlike white or unbleached flour.

Whole Wheat Pastry Flour is best used for baking cakes or cookies. It is a very light flour, and comes from the wheat berry with a low gluten content. It contains all the vitamins and nutrients found in wheat. Make sure to use whole wheat pastry flour when it is called for in a recipe, as opposed to regular whole wheat flour. This is a much lighter flour than whole wheat flour.

The Great Controversy

Best-seller on history and Bible prophecy.

Lessons of Love

Beautiful devotional on Christ's parables.

The Answer Book

Dozens of Bible topics in this Q&A study book.

Habits That Heal

Explore America's longest-living culture.

Happiness for Life

Small book on developing your walk with God.

Simply Fresh

Simple, delicious, recipes your family will love!

Story Time

True stories that teach character-building lessons.

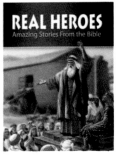

Real Heroes

Stories of the great heroes in the Old Testament.

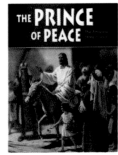

The Prince of Peace

Covers the life of Jesus from His birth to Calvary.

Also Available...

Many of these titles are avaiable in Spanish!

Contact details on next page.

FEATURED BOOK

The Promise of Peace

This devotional book takes a broad look at the plan of salvation by starting with the ever-important question "Why was sin permitted?" It provides deep, meaningful encouragement for those who seek peace in an increasingly chaotic world.

Call 1 (888) 661-4569 to learn more

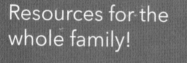
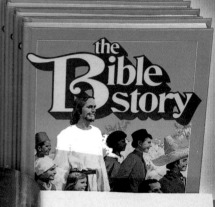